WISCONSIN

COOK BOOK

Compiled and edited
by
Karin Marple Wade

GOLDEN
WEST
PUBLISHERS

Front cover photo courtesy of National Pork Producers Council
Back cover photo courtesy of Wisconsin Milk Marketing Board

Printed in the United States of America

2nd printing ® 2002

ISBN #1-885590-41-5

Golden West Publishers, Inc.
4113 N. Longview Ave.
Phoenix, AZ 85014, USA

(602) 265-4392

Table of Contents

(Continued on next page)

Table of Contents (continued)

Breads

Desserts

Wisconsin!

Welcome to "America's Dairyland" and the finest collection of recipes, contributed by the residents of this great state, that you will find anywhere. From *Wisconsin Gouda & Beer Spread* to *Polish Molasses Cookies,* these truly unique recipes reflect the ethnic makeup and culture of the early pioneers as well as the current favorites of homemakers, chefs, bed and breakfast owners, gourmet cooks and many more.

Enjoy these tastes of Wisconsin!

Wisconsin Facts

Size – 26th largest state with an area of 56,154 square miles
Population – 5,170,000
Statehood – May 29, 1848 – 30th state
State Song – "On Wisconsin"
State Nickname – Badger State (unofficial)
State Motto – Forward!
State Bird – Robin
State Flower – Wood Violet
State Tree – Sugar Maple
State Fish – Muskellunge (Muskie)
State Animal – Badger
State Insect – Honeybee
State Wildlife Animal – White-tailed deer
State Domestic Animal – Dairy cow
State Fossil – Trilobite

Famous Folks from Wisconsin

Georgia O'Keeffe, one of the leading artists of our time
Frank Lloyd Wright, arguably the world's greatest architect
Thornton Wilder, Pulitzer prize-winning author
Spencer Tracy, born and raised in Milwaukee
Gary Burghoff, MASH's Radar O'Reilly
Harry Houdini, raised in Appleton
Liberace, born and raised in Milwaukee, was one of the world's most famous pianists

Other fun facts about Wisconsin

Nearly 21 million gallons of ice cream are sold in Wisconsin each year • The first ice cream sundae was concocted in Two Rivers in 1881 • The Ringling Brothers of circus fame were from Baraboo (home of the Circus World Museum) • Each year, the EAA Fly-In brings 12,000 planes to Oshkosh, making it the busiest airport in the world • Door County has more shoreline than any other county in the U.S. (more than 250 miles) • The American Birkebeiner, the largest cross-country ski race in the U.S., brings nearly 7,000 competitors to Cable • Green Bay, home of the Packers is known as "Titletown USA" • Sheboygan is the "Bratwurst Capital" of the world • Bellville and Elmwood claim to be the UFO Capitals of the world.

• • •

Learn more about Wisconsin by calling 1-800-432-8747, or visit Wisconsin's internet site at: tourism.state.wi.us

APPETIZERS & BEVERAGES

Wisconsin-Style Appetizers

Faye Bonnin, (one of the first women in America to own and operate a jewelry store) advises that the folks in Wisconsin would prefer to let their mouths water waiting for a sumptuous meal than fuss over appetizers. But, on the rare occasion that they do serve them, they often consist of the following.

Faye Bonnin—Guild Jewelers, Appleton

Glasses of DOOR COUNTY CHERRY WINE
Platters of CRACKERS and WISCONSIN CHEESE CURDS
THURINGER SAUSAGE, cut into bite-size pieces
SUMMER SAUSAGE, cut into bite-size pieces
CELERY stuffed with CREAM CHEESE, sprinkled with PAPRIKA and cut diagonally
CARROT STICKS
BREAD STICKS

Swiss Cheese Fondue

"Fondue, the French word for 'melt', is a classic dish of Swiss heritage. This is one of the recipes brought to America by my Swiss ancestors."

Marian B. Karlen—Monroe

1 lb. SWISS CHEESE, coarsely grated
1 Tbsp. CORNSTARCH
1/2 tsp. SALT
1/4 tsp. WHITE PEPPER
1/4 tsp. NUTMEG
2 cups BUTTERMILK
1 clove GARLIC
1 loaf FRENCH BREAD, cubed

In a bowl, toss cheese with cornstarch, salt, pepper and nutmeg. In fondue pot, over low heat, heat buttermilk and add garlic clove. When mixture is hot, remove the garlic and add the cheese mixture. Heat and stir constantly until cheese is melted. Serve from fondue pot, over a lighted burner, dipping cubes of French bread with long-handled fondue forks.

Monroe

"Our county was named Green County because of the rolling hills which reminded our ancestors of their homeland. Those early immigrants continued their farming and cheesemaking here in America. Many of their wonderful recipes are still prepared today in our restaurants as well as our kitchens. In the summer, our county festivals reflect that heritage."

Marian B. Karlen

Shiitake Hazelnut Paté

Not long ago Shiitake (She-tah-key) mushrooms were reserved for use only by Emperors, and fiercely guarded by Samurai warriors. Now this imperial treasure is growing in America—carefully cultivated on natural hardwood logs in the true oriental tradition.

John Cook—Shiitake Growers Assn. of Wisconsin, Birchwood

4 oz. SHIITAKE MUSHROOMS
3 Tbsp. BUTTER
1 clove GARLIC, minced
1/8 tsp. THYME
1/4 tsp. SALT
1/8 tsp. PEPPER
1 tsp. fresh PARSLEY LEAVES
1/4 cup toasted HAZELNUTS
3 oz. NEUFCHÂTEL CHEESE
2 tsp. DRY SHERRY

Trim and discard woody ends from mushroom stems. In food processor, finely chop mushroom caps and stems. In a medium skillet, melt butter. Add mushrooms and garlic and sauté 5 minutes. Stir in thyme, salt and pepper. In food processor, chop parsley. Add hazelnuts and process. Add Neufchâtel cheese and process until smooth. Add sherry and mushroom mixture. Process until well mixed. Spread or mold in serving dish. Cover. Chill at least 1 hour. Serve with crackers.

Yields 1 cup.

Quick Paté

Janet Nordström Brooks—Oshkosh

14 oz. GROUND ROUND
10 oz. BRAUNSCHWEIGER
1 YELLOW ONION, finely chopped
1 clove GARLIC, pressed
2 Tbsp. SWAN® POTATO FLOUR
1 tsp. SALT
1 tsp. BLACK PEPPER
2 EGGS
3/4 cup HALF and HALF
1 Tbsp. SHERRY or BRANDY

Place all ingredients in a food processor and mix well. Oil a bread pan, place mixture in pan and bake for 75 minutes at 350°. Test with a toothpick for doneness. Let cool and store in refrigerator (wrapped in foil), at least overnight. Can be frozen for 2 to 3 months.

Mini Calzones

(Stuffed Sandwich)

This recipe created by the "Ask Addie" columnist and food writer for "The Reporter", Fond du Lac and "The Lakeland Times", Minocqua.

Adeline Halfmann—Arbor Vitae

1 lb. frozen ITALIAN BREAD AND PIZZA DOUGH
4 hot ITALIAN SAUSAGES, skinned, diced
4 oz. fresh MUSHROOMS, coarsely chopped
1/2 cup chopped RED or GREEN BELL PEPPER
1/2 cup chopped ONION
1 tsp. minced GARLIC
1/2 cup chopped BLACK OLIVES
1/2 tsp. dried OREGANO LEAVES, crumbled
1/2 tsp. ground FENNEL SEED
4 oz. FONTINA or PROVOLONE CHEESE, grated
4 oz. shredded MOZZARELLA CHEESE
1/4 tsp. freshly ground BLACK PEPPER
SALT to taste
1 large EGG, beaten
1 Tbsp. WATER
2 Tbsp. YELLOW CORNMEAL

Thaw bread dough, loosely covered with plastic wrap, to room temperature and pliable (4-5 hours). Divide dough into 18 pieces, shaping each into a ball; let rest 10 minutes for easier rolling. On a lightly floured surface, flatten each ball into 2-inch rounds; roll each round into a 3 1/2 to 4-inch circle and cover with a clean towel.

Preheat oven to 375°. In a 10-inch skillet over medium heat, brown sausages, breaking up with a spoon until finely crumbled; drain and discard drippings. Add mushrooms, pepper, onion and garlic to the skillet; cook and stir until onions are glossy, about 3 minutes; let cool. When cool, add olives, oregano, fennel seed, cheeses and pepper; mix thoroughly. Taste; if necessary, add salt. Spread about 2 tablespoons filling on lower half of each dough circle, leaving a half-inch border around the edges.

(Continued on next page)

Mini-Calzones (continued from previous page)

In a small bowl, whisk together egg and water to make an egg wash. Brush edges of each circle then fold over to make a half-circle. Seal edges tightly with tines of a fork that has been dipped in flour. Prick tops of each calzone with a fork to make steam vents; brush tops with egg wash. Place calzones on 2 baking sheets that have been sprinkled with the cornmeal. Bake in preheated oven about 15 minutes, or until calzones are crisp and brown. Serve hot. Makes 18 appetizers.

Lake Superior Whitefish Livers

Ruth Grubbe—The Village Inn, Cornucopia

2 lbs. fresh WHITEFISH LIVERS
2 cups SEASONED FLOUR (see below)
1 1/2 cups BUTTER
3 cups diced ONION
3 cups diced GREEN BELL PEPPER

Roll livers in seasoned flour and set aside. Heat 3/4 cup butter in a large skillet over medium-high heat. When hot (test drop of water should sizzle) add livers individually and gently brown by tossing. Add onions and green peppers. Continue to toss gently as onions become translucent. Add remainder of butter, as needed, throughout the cooking time. Serve on small plates garnished with parsley and lemon wedges.

Seasoned Flour

2 cups FLOUR
2 Tbsp. SEASONED SALT
2 Tbsp. GARLIC SALT
1/2 tsp. WHITE PEPPER

Combine all ingredients and mix thoroughly.

Salmon Party Log

Sally Teresinski—Wisconsin Czechs Inc.
(Vařte S Námi Cook Book), Oshkosh

1 can (16 oz.) SALMON (2 cups)
1 pkg. (8 oz.) CREAM CHEESE, softened
1 Tbsp. LEMON JUICE
2 tsp. grated ONION
1 tsp. HORSERADISH
1/4 tsp. SALT
1/4 tsp. LIQUID SMOKE
1/2 cup PECANS
3 Tbsp. chopped PARSLEY

Drain and flake salmon. Remove skin and bones. Combine salmon and next 6 ingredients. Mix well. Chill several hours. Shape salmon mixture into a log shape and roll in combined pecan and parsley mixture. Place in the center of a serving dish on a bed of lettuce leaves and garnish with additional parsley.

Baraboo

The five sons of a German harnessmaker who lived in Baraboo founded the circus that became the Ringling Bros. Circus (and later, the Ringling Bros. and Barnum & Baily Circus.) Their first performance in 1882 was known as "Classic and Comic Concert Company". The Circus World Museum in Baraboo offers big-top circus performances, parades and more during the summer season.

Stormy's Shrimp Dip

Matilda "Stormy" Bobula—Baraboo

1 env. PLAIN GELATIN
1/4 cup WATER
1 can (10.75 oz.) TOMATO SOUP
2 pkgs. (8 oz. ea.) CREAM CHEESE
1 cup SALAD DRESSING
3/4 cup chopped ONION
3/4 cup chopped CELERY
2 cans (4 oz. ea.) TINY SHRIMP

Dissolve gelatin in water. Combine with other ingredients. Allow to set in refrigerator. When ready to serve, place dip in serving dish and serve with crackers of your choice.

Wisconsin Gouda & Beer Spread

Wisconsin Milk Marketing Board—Madison

1 ball (2 lbs.) WISCONSIN GOUDA CHEESE*
3/4 cup BUTTER, cubed and softened
2 Tbsp. snipped fresh CHIVES
2 Tsp. DIJON MUSTARD
1/2 cup amber or dark BEER, room temperature
COCKTAIL RYE or PUMPERNICKEL BREAD slices

Cut 1/5 off the top of the cheese ball and remove the center of the ball, leaving a 1/2-inch thick shell. Shred enough of the cheese removed from the ball and the top to measure 4 cups. Reserve remaining cheese for another use.

In a large bowl, place shredded cheese, butter, chives and mustard; mix with a spoon until blended. Stir in beer until blended. Return the cheese mixture to the hollowed cheese ball and chill until serving time. Serve with rye or pumpernickel slices.

*Note: Wisconsin Edam can be substituted for Gouda. If cheese is not available in ball form, this spread may be served in your favorite serving bowl.

Madison

Madison became the territorial capital in 1836 and the state capital in 1848. The University of Wisconsin was established here in 1848. Surrounded by the "Four Lakes of Madison" (Mendota, Monona, Wingra and Waubesa), Madison is a thriving cultural center of the state and serves as a trade center for a rich agricultural region. The 2,500-ton, 286-foot high dome of the capital building, by ordinance, dominates the skyline.

Bacon Almond Dip

Sally Teresinski—Wisconsin Czechs Inc.
(Dobré Chutnán'i! Cook Book), Oshkosh

1 lb. BACON
2 pkgs. (3 oz. ea.) CREAM CHEESE with CHIVES, room temperature
1 cup SOUR CREAM
2 Tbsp. CHILI SAUCE
1/4 tsp. TABASCO® SAUCE
Freshly ground PEPPER, to taste
1/4 cup chopped GREEN ONIONS
1/2 cup slivered ALMONDS, toasted

In a large skillet, cook bacon over moderate heat until crisp, drain on paper towels and when cool, crumble and set aside. In a food processor (or bowl), combine cream cheese, sour cream, chili sauce, tabasco and pepper. Add onion, bacon and almonds and process (or mix) until blended, but still chunky. Remove to serving bowl and refrigerate until ready to serve. Can be refrigerated for 2 days, or frozen and defrosted in refrigerator.

Stuffed Shiitake

John Cook—Shiitake Growers Assn. of Wisconsin, Birchwood

1 lb. fresh SHIITAKE MUSHROOMS
1/2 cup BUTTER, melted
SALT and PEPPER to taste
1 cup chopped ONION
1/4 cup diced HAM
3/4 tsp. THYME
1 Tbsp. DRY SHERRY
1 1/2 cups HEAVY CREAM
PARMESAN CHEESE

Sort 12 large shiitake caps. Brush gills with butter, and season with salt and pepper, set aside. Chop remaining shiitake– including stems. Combine remaining butter, onion, ham and thyme. Add chopped mushrooms and sherry. Cover and cook over moderate heat for 2 minutes. Add cream and cook on high for 5 minutes. Spoon mixture into shiitake caps and sprinkle with Parmesan cheese. Bake on top rack of 375° preheated oven for 15-20 minutes.

Lemon-Orange Slush

"This is a good ladies' drink for Holiday parties."

Lois Dorschner—Waupaca

2 cups SUGAR
7 cups WATER
4 BAGS GREEN TEA
1/2 cup HOT WATER
1 can (12 oz.) LEMONADE
1 can (12 oz.) ORANGE JUICE
2 cups GIN
7-Up® or CITRUS SODA of choice

In a saucepan, combine sugar and water. Bring to a boil and then cool. Add tea bags to 1/2 cup hot water. Allow to steep and then cool. Combine balance of ingredients with cooled sugar water and tea and freeze. When ready to serve, place a scoop of slush in a glass and add 7-Up or your favorite citrus soda. Garnish rims of glasses with slices of orange. Slush will keep in freezer for several months.

Three Lakes Wine Punch

Maureen McCain—Three Lakes Winery, Three Lakes

1 can (6 oz.) each frozen:
CRANBERRY JUICE COCKTAIL CONCENTRATE
ORANGE JUICE CONCENTRATE
PINEAPPLE JUICE CONCENTRATE
1 bottle (750 mil.) THREE LAKES® CRANBERRY WINE
3 bottles (10 oz. ea.) CARBONATED WATER

Thaw concentrates and mix in a 3 quart pitcher. Cover and chill. To serve, add wine and carbonated water; mix well. Serve over ice. Makes 16 (6 oz.) servings.

Legends say that the cranberry, as traditional as apple pie, was served at the first Thanksgiving dinner. The Eastern Indians called the cranberry "sassamanesh". They considered the bright, tangy, wild berry a symbol of peace.

Egg Coffee

"My parents were of Irish and German descent, and before every meal they had to have the best cup of coffee! An invitation to dinner was also an invitation for comment, as we wended our way home, on the merits, if any, of the host's coffee."

Norma E. Pensis—Green Bay

8 cups WATER
1 EGG, washed
8 Tbsp. COFFEE, coarse grind

In a granite coffee pot (insides removed), bring water to a rolling boil. Break the egg into a bowl and then add the shells to the bowl. Add the coffee grounds to the egg and stir (you may need to add a little water in order to mix well). Add the coffee mixture to the coffee pot and stir. Continue boiling for 5 minutes. Turn heat to warm and add a few ice cubes (this settles the coffee grounds). Strain if desired. Serve in mugs with sugar and cream as desired.

Strawberry-Orange Summer Freeze

Lynn M. Irvine—1st Place, 6th Annual Wis. Berry Recipe Contest, Racine

1 qt. fresh STRAWBERRIES
5 lg. ORANGES
1 med. LEMON
1 LIME
4-5 cups crushed ICE

Clean and hull strawberries. Squeeze juice from oranges, lemon and lime. Place juice in a blender. Add strawberries and blend until smooth. Add crushed ice (one cup at a time) and blend until mixture is fairly smooth. Pour into glasses and garnish with a whole strawberry.

Cranberry Mixed Drink Recipes

Each recipe serves one person.

Northland Cranberries, Inc.—Wisconsin Rapids

Fall Down & Go Boom

1 oz. LIGHT RUM
1/2 oz. DARK RUM
1 tsp. SUGAR
2 oz. CRANBERRY JUICE
2 Tbsp. LEMON JUICE
2 Tbsp. LIME JUICE
1 EGG WHITE
CRUSHED ICE

Combine all ingredients in a shaker and strain into chilled glass over ice.

Flying Saucer

2 oz. GRAPEFRUIT JUICE
1 oz. ORANGE JUICE
1 oz. CRANBERRY JUICE
1 tsp. HONEY
3 oz. GINGER ALE

Mix honey with a small amount of hot water before combining with balance of ingredients. Pour into chilled glass over ice.

Naked Berry

2 oz. PLAIN YOGURT
5 oz. CRANBERRY JUICE
1 oz. LEMON JUICE
1 tsp. SUGAR

Place all ingredients in blender with ice. Blend until smooth. Serve over ice in chilled glass.

Red Passion

1 oz. VODKA
3 oz. CRANBERRY JUICE
1/2 oz. PINEAPPLE JUICE
2 tsp. SUGAR

Combine and pour over ice in tall, chilled glass. Garnish with pineapple wedges and cherries.

Wisconsin Delight

2 oz. VODKA
5 oz. CRANBERRY JUICE

Combine ingredients and pour over ice in tall, chilled glass.

Desert Shield

1 oz. VODKA
3 oz. CRANBERRY JUICE
1/2 oz. PINEAPPLE JUICE
2 tsp. SUGAR

Combine all ingredients and pour into tall chilled glass over ice. Garnish with lime wedge.

Karoff

1 1/2 oz. VODKA
1 oz. CRANBERRY JUICE
5 oz. SELTZER

Combine all ingredients and pour into tall chilled glass over ice. Garnish with lime wedge.

Woo-Woo

1 1/2 oz. VODKA
1/2 oz. PEACH SCHNAPPS
4 oz. CRANBERRY JUICE

Combine all ingredients and pour into tall chilled glass over ice. Garnish with orange wedge and a cherry.

Flawless Ruby

1 oz. DARK RUM
1 oz. LIGHT RUM
DASH OF BITTERS
3 oz. CRANBERRY JUICE
1 oz. ORANGE JUICE

Combine all ingredients and pour into tall chilled glass over ice. Garnish with orange wedge and a cherry.

Madras Plaid

1 1/2 oz. VODKA
2 oz. CRANBERRY JUICE
2 oz. ORANGE JUICE

Combine all ingredients and pour into tall chilled glass over ice. Garnish with orange wedge and a cherry.

Lake Superior Breeze

1 1/2 oz. VODKA
2 oz. GRAPEFRUIT JUICE
3 oz. CRANBERRY JUICE

Combine all ingredients and pour into tall chilled glass over ice. Garnish with orange wedge and a cherry.

Sex on a Beach

1 oz. VODKA
1 oz. PEACH SCHNAPPS
2 oz. ORANGE JUICE
2 oz. CRANBERRY JUICE

Combine all ingredients and pour into tall chilled glass over ice. Garnish with orange wedge and a cherry.

Note: Try Southern Comfort® instead of vodka or strawberry schnapps instead of the peach schnapps.

Norwegian Toast

"Being of Scandinavian heritage, just about everyone in my family is a great coffee drinker. Foods that required 'dunking' were especially favored. This recipe is perfect for that purpose!"

Betty Gayle Carlson—Siskiwit Lake

1 cup BUTTER
1 1/2 cups SUGAR
2 EGGS
1 cup SOUR CREAM
1 tsp. BAKING SODA
4 cups FLOUR
chopped ALMONDS or WALNUTS

Combine ingredients in order given. Batter will be thick and sticky and does not rise much (don't be discouraged). Shape into three loaves and place crosswise on a cookie sheet. Bake at 350° for 35 to 40 minutes. Remove from oven and cut loaves into 1/2" slices. Place slices on cookie sheets, return to 350° oven and toast until golden brown (about 7 minutes per side).

Cran-Raspberry Brunch Cake

Lori Spindler—Warrens Cranberry Festival, Warrens

3 cups ALL-PURPOSE FLOUR, sifted
2 1/2 tsp. BAKING POWDER
1/2 tsp. SALT
1 cup (2 sticks) BUTTER, softened
1 1/2 cups SUGAR
1 tsp. VANILLA EXTRACT
4 EGGS
3 ctn. (12 oz. ea.) CRANBERRY-RASPBERRY CRAN-FRUIT®
whole fresh CRANBERRIES and RASPBERRIES
MINT LEAVES

Preheat oven to 350°. Sift flour, baking powder and salt together; set aside. In a large mixing bowl, combine butter, sugar and vanilla. Using an electric mixer, beat on high speed until creamy. Add eggs, one at a time, beating well after each addition. Gradually add dry ingredients to batter, mixing well. Spread 2/3 of batter in a greased 15 1/2 x 10 1/2 jellyroll pan. Spread Cran-Fruit evenly on top. Spoon 12 mounds of remaining batter over Cran-Fruit; flatten slightly. Bake 30-35 minutes until golden brown. Drizzle with ***Almond Icing*** and garnish with cranberries, raspberries and mint leaves.

Almond Icing

1 tsp. BUTTER
2 Tbsp. MILK
1 1/2 cups POWDERED SUGAR
1/2 tsp. ALMOND EXTRACT

In a small glass bowl, combine butter and milk. Microwave on high for 30-45 seconds until hot. Add powdered sugar and almond extract; stir until smooth. Using a teaspoon, drizzle over hot brunch cake.

Note: One-half cup fresh or frozen blueberries may be added to Cran-Fruit for an interesting variation.

All Wisconsin Scrambled Omelet Prepared in the Big Fry Pan!

"The Big Fry Pan is 54" in diameter, 6" deep and has a handle that is 54" long. I use an 18" spatula to stir the omelets and a dust pan to serve it up with. I travel with the Big Fry Pan to many events throughout the state and serve this omelet to all."

Bob Williams—Wisconsin Department of Agriculture, Madison

1/2 lb. BUTTER
3 cups chopped ONIONS
6 cups chopped MUSHROOMS
2 Tbsp. CHICKEN BOUILLON GRANULES
6 lbs. diced HAM
250 EGGS, beaten
6 lbs. shredded CHEESE (sharp cheddar, Swiss, Monterey Jack or other favorite)
2 Tbsp. SALT
3 Tbsp. PEPPER

Melt butter in skillet over moderate heat. Sauté onions and mushrooms. Stir in chicken bouillon. Add ham and allow to warm. Add eggs. When mixture is partially set, stir in shredded cheese. When cheese is melted and while mixture is still moist, remove from pan and serve.

Serves 100

Apricot Stuffed French Toast

"My nieces told me of a pajama party treat that they had enjoyed. I changed the presentation somewhat and now use this recipe to delight guests at the Hillcrest."

Gayle Hohner—The Hillcrest Inn & Carriage House, Burlington

1 loaf WHITE BREAD
1 jar APRICOT JAM
8 oz. CREAM CHEESE
4 EGGS
1/2 cup CREAM
POWDERED SUGAR
NUTMEG

Combine jam and cheese, and make sandwiches. Beat eggs and cream together. Dip sandwiches into egg mixture and fry until golden brown. Serve topped with powdered sugar and nutmeg. Garnish with fresh fruit and sizzling sausages. Serve with maple syrup on the side.

Spinach Soufflé

"This recipe has something a little different for you to try, an emu egg (or, 3 large chicken eggs will do)!"

Eleanor Howarth—Phil & Eleanor's Steak House, Medford

3 Tbsp. OLIVE OIL
3 Tbsp. FLOUR
1/4 tsp. SALT
1/8 tsp. PEPPER
1 cup MILK
3 Tbsp. finely chopped ONION
2 cloves GARLIC, pressed
1 tsp. chopped HOT PEPPER
1 cup cooked SPINACH, chopped
1 EMU EGG, separated
1/2 cup RICOTTA CHEESE

In a saucepan, heat oil. Gradually blend in flour, salt, pepper, milk, onion, garlic and pepper. Cook, stirring constantly until mixture thickens. Press as much liquid from spinach as possible and add to flour mixture. Add beaten emu egg yolk. Beat emu egg white until stiff. Fold egg white and cheese into the flour mixture. Pour all into a well-greased casserole dish. Place casserole in a larger pan containing hot water and bake in a moderate 350° oven for 45 to 50 minutes or until golden brown.

Kolaches

"Kolaches are an Easter tradition in our family. This recipe was passed down from my grandmother Mary Noskowiak. It is Bohemian in origin, as is our heritage. Easter morning breakfast includes kolaches, kielbasa sausage and boiled eggs. It is a tradition that I hope will continue for many generations to come."

Mary Jo Noskowiak Stefanescu—Racine

1 3/4 cup MILK
1/2 cup SHORTENING
1/2 cup SUGAR
1/2 cup MASHED POTATOES

Mix the above ingredients in a saucepan and heat to scalding. Set aside to cool to lukewarm.

1 pkg. (4 oz.) ACTIVE DRY YEAST
1/2 cup WARM WATER

When milk mixture is lukewarm, sprinkle yeast over warm water, mix to dissolve. Let set until bubbly then combine with the milk mixture. Add:

2 EGGS, slightly beaten
1 tsp. SALT

Mix well and gradually add and knead in:

6 1/2 to 7 cups FLOUR

When a soft dough is achieved, knead well on a floured surface. Place dough in a large greased bowl, cover with a towel and let rise until double in size. Punch down to remove excess air. Take walnut-size pieces of dough and roll in hand to ball shape. Place on greased cookie sheets, about 12 to a pan. Press each ball slightly to flatten. Use a small, flat-bottomed glass to press an indentation into the center of each kolache. Fill with about 1 1/2 teaspoons filling of your choice (cherry, apricot, prune, poppyseed, strawberry etc.). Bake on middle rack of preheated 350° oven until edges and bottoms are golden. Place kolaches on racks and cool. Store in airtight containers.

Cheryl's Baked French Toast

"My father traveled throughout Wisconsin for several years as a salesman. He knew all of the best places to eat, but always said that this was his favorite breakfast of all. It is also very popular with our guests at Country Woods."

Cheryl A. Carlson—Country Woods Bed & Breakfast, Ellison Bay

1 baguette FRENCH BREAD, cut into 1" slices
6 lg. EGGS
1 1/2 cups MILK
1 cup CREAM
1 tsp. VANILLA EXTRACT
1/4 tsp. ground CINNAMON
1/4 tsp. ground NUTMEG
1/4 cup BUTTER, melted
1/2 cup LIGHT BROWN SUGAR
1 Tbsp. LIGHT CORN SYRUP
1/2 cup sliced ALMONDS or PECANS
MAPLE SYRUP, warmed

Lightly oil a 9 x 13 baking pan. Arrange bread slices, overlapping, to fill pan. In medium-size bowl, combine eggs, milk, cream, vanilla, cinnamon and nutmeg. Beat well. Pour over bread slices. Cover and refrigerate overnight.

Preheat oven to 350°. In a small bowl, combine the butter, sugar and corn syrup. Spread evenly over bread. Sprinkle with nuts and bake for 40 minutes. Serve with warm maple syrup.

Serves 6 to 8.

Swiss Crème Omelet

"Not having the ingredients I needed to make a quick breakfast for unexpected guests, I created this recipe out of necessity."

Lisa Rudolph—Oshkosh Public Library, Oshkosh

1/2 cup ASPARAGUS, chopped
3 EGGS
2 Tbsp. WATER
SALT and PEPPER to taste
1/4 cup OLIVE OIL
1 clove GARLIC, minced
1 tsp. LEMON JUICE
1/2 cup SOUR CREAM
1/2 cup shredded SWISS CHEESE, divided

Cook asparagus until just tender. Whisk eggs and water with salt and pepper. Heat olive oil in a skillet and sauté garlic until golden. Pour in egg mixture and cook until lightly set. Cover. Combine lemon juice with sour cream. Add asparagus, sour cream and most of the Swiss cheese to one side of the omelet. Fold other side over filled portion and sprinkle with balance of the Swiss cheese. Heat until cheese melts and serve.

Oshkosh

Because of extensive sawmill operations, Oshkosh was dubbed "Sawdust City". Between 1859 and 1875, downtown Oshkosh was destroyed by fire four times. After the last fire, rebuilding was done using brick. Over 240 acres of parks and the University of Wisconsin-Oshkosh campus are only two of the features for which this city is noted. Another is the Experimental Aircraft Association's Air Adventure Museum and their International Fly-In which is held the first week of August. The Paine Art Center, Oshkosh Public Museum, Grand Opera House and Menominee Park Zoo are favorite attractions of both residents and visitors alike.

Creamed Eggs on Toast

Don De Clerc—Green Bay

12 HARD-BOILED EGGS, separated

White Sauce:
2 Tbsp. BUTTER
3 Tbsp. FLOUR
1 cup MILK
1/4 tsp. SALT
1/8 tsp. PEPPER

Chop egg whites and set aside. Push egg yolks through a wire mesh strainer into a bowl. Set aside. In a saucepan, melt butter, add the flour and combine. Add milk, salt and pepper. When sauce has thickened, add chopped egg whites. Heat well. Serve over toast or muffins with egg yolks sprinkled on top.

German Potato Pancakes

"This recipe was given to me by my mother, Lucille Schmidt."

Ruth Evans—Neenah

6 lg. POTATOES, grated
3 EGGS
1 tsp. SALT
3 Tbsp. FLOUR
4 slices BACON, cut into 1/2" strips

Combine potatoes, eggs, salt and flour. Make patties of potato mixture and place in skillet with a small amount of oil. Lay 2 to 3 strips of bacon on top. Cook patties until golden brown, turn and cook the other side. Serve with butter, applesauce or syrup.

Wisconsin Wild Rice Soup

"Wild rice is grown throughout Wisconsin and is a favorite addition to many meals."

Jeanine Jacobs—Antigo

1/2 cup WILD RICE
1 qt. plus 3 cups CHICKEN BROTH, divided
1/2 cup LONG GRAIN WHITE RICE
1/2 cup BUTTER
16 oz. MUSHROOMS
1 cup chopped ONION
1 cup chopped CELERY
MILK
SALT and PEPPER to taste

Wash wild rice, place in a saucepan and add 1 1/2 cups chicken broth. Cook for about 1 hour or until rice is tender. Add more water if needed. In another saucepan, cook the white rice in 1 1/2 cups chicken broth about 20 minutes, or until tender. In a large Dutch oven, sauté mushrooms, onion and celery in butter for about 8 minutes. Add 1 quart of chicken broth and the wild and white rice. Add enough milk to make a good soup. Thicken soup slightly with flour mixed with broth. Add salt and pepper to taste.

Serves 8.

Whitefish Soup

"Fresh Lake Superior whitefish is enjoyed in many ways by Wisconsinites who live along Lake Superior's south shores. This hearty soup is especially good during our long cold winters and after snowmobiling, cross country skiing, dog sledding or ice fishing."

Betty Artlip—Cornucopia

1/2 lg. GREEN BELL PEPPER, cut into 1" pieces
3 Tbsp. chopped ONION
1 clove GARLIC, minced
2 Tbsp. BUTTER, MARGARINE or COOKING OIL
1 can (16 oz.) diced TOMATOES
1 can (8 oz.) TOMATO SAUCE
3/4 cup DRY RED WINE
3 Tbsp. fresh snipped PARSLEY
1/2 tsp. SALT
1/4 tsp. OREGANO
1/4 tsp. BASIL
1/4 tsp. PEPPER
1/8 tsp. ROSEMARY
1 lb. fresh WHITEFISH FILLETS

Sauté green pepper, onion and garlic in butter then stir in next nine ingredients. Bring to a rolling boil. Reduce heat and simmer for 20 minutes. Cut whitefish into bite-size pieces, add to sautéed ingredients and bring to a boil. Simmer, stirring occasionally, for 7 to 10 minutes or until fish flakes easily.

Lake Superior

Lake Superior is the deepest of the five Great Lakes of North America, and the largest body of freshwater in the world. The lake covers 31,700 square miles, with a length of 350 miles and width of 160 miles. Northeastern Wisconsin shares over 290 miles of sandy shoreline with this giant, including the Apostle Islands north of Ashland where the beautiful Madeline Island can be found. In 1975 the sinking of the S.S. Edmund Fitzgerald in Lake Superior, with 29 men aboard, prompted Gordon Lightfoot to write and sing the haunting "Wreck of the Edmund Fitzgerald".

Fresh Tomato Soup

"My husband taught me how to make this soup the way his mother made it!"

Nancy Robaidek—Krakow

1 med. ONION, sliced
1 Tbsp. BUTTER
4 med. TOMATOES, peeled and cut into large chunks
2 Tbsp. SUGAR
EGG DUMPLINGS
2 Tbsp. SOUR CREAM

Sauté onions in butter until tranlucent, add tomatoes and sugar. Simmer 15 minutes. Add ***Egg Dumplings*** and sour cream and serve immediately.

Egg Dumplings

1 med. EGG, beaten
1 Tbsp. WATER
1/2 tsp. SALT
1/3 cup FLOUR

Combine all ingredients well. Drop by teaspoonful into boiling water, boil 1 minute, drain and add to soup.

Potato Cheese Soup

"I created this soup in the 50's for my children and it is still their favorite."

Jeanine Jacobs—Antigo

2 qts. POTATOES, peeled and diced
1 cup finely chopped ONIONS
2 heaping Tbsp. CHICKEN SOUP BASE
1/2 lb. AMERICAN CHEESE
1 qt. MILK
6 slices BACON, fried crisp and crumbled
chopped CHIVES or PARSLEY

Place potatoes, onions and chicken soup base in a large saucepan and cover with water. Cook until potatoes are almost done. Using a slotted spoon, remove half of the potatoes, mash and return to saucepan. Break cheese into chunks and add to mixture. When cheese has melted add milk, bacon and chives. Bring to a simmer and heat through.

Makes 6 servings.

Boiled Tomato Soup

"When I was a caterer in the Oconomowoc area, I received this recipe from one of my clients. It was a favorite at her bridge luncheons."

Carol A. Beilke—Oconomowoc

1 stick BUTTER
1 lg. ONION, sliced
1/2 tsp. DILLWEED
1 1/2 tsp. THYME
1/2 tsp. BASIL
1 can (28 oz.) ITALIAN PLUM TOMATOES, quartered
1 can (15 oz.) ITALIAN PLUM TOMATOES, quartered
3 Tbsp. TOMATO PASTE
1/4 cup FLOUR
3 3/4 cups CHICKEN BROTH
3 tsp. SUGAR
1 1/2 tsp. SALT
1/4 tsp. WHITE PEPPER
fresh CHIVES or DILL
1 cup HEAVY CREAM, whipped
1/2 cup grated PARMESAN CHEESE

In a 4 or 5-quart saucepan, melt butter and add onion and herbs. Sauté until onions are just soft. Add tomatoes and tomato paste. Simmer for 10 minutes stirring occasionally. Combine flour with 1/2 cup of chicken broth and stir until smooth. Add to saucepan with remaining broth. Heat to just below boiling and simmer for 25 minutes. Add sugar, salt and pepper.*

When cool, blend mixture in small portions in blender until smooth. Place in a saucepan and heat. Pour soup into serving bowls, top with a sprinkle of chives or dill and a spoonful of whipped cream. Sprinkle Parmesan cheese on top.

*At this point, soup may be cooled and either refrigerated or frozen for later use.

Did you know?

In 1856, the first kindergarten in the United States was opened in Watertown.

Czarning with Kluski

(Duck Soup with Potato Dumplings)

"Traditionally, duck soup was made with the blood of the duck, however, I have substituted Kitchen Bouquet for the blood to make it more modern and I don't think the flavor is lost. Either the entire duck or just the unused pieces and parts of one may be used in this recipe."

Phyllis Reinert—Two Rivers

1 DUCK
1 stalk CELERY, diced
1 sm. ONION, sliced
3-4 whole ALLSPICE
3-4 whole CLOVES
2-3 BAY LEAVES
SALT to taste
1/4 tsp. PEPPER
15 dried PRUNES
1/2 cup RAISINS
1 APPLE, diced
3 Tbsp. FLOUR
1 Tbsp. KITCHEN BOUQUET®
1/2 cup SUGAR
1/2 cup VINEGAR

Place duck in a large saucepan and cover with water. Bring to a boiling point. Skim fat from surface of water. Add celery and onion. Place allspice, cloves and bay leaves in a cloth bag and add to saucepan. Cook slowly until meat is almost done (about 2 hours). Remove bag of spices and add fruit. Cook for about 1/2 hour longer. Combine flour with 3/4 cup soup stock and the Kitchen Bouquet. Stir until smooth and pour into soup, stirring constantly. Add sugar and vinegar and bring back to boiling point to heat thoroughly. When serving, add ***Potato Dumplings*** to each soup bowl.

Potato Dumplings

2 cups raw POTATOES
2 EGGS, beaten
1 tsp. SALT
1/2-2 cups FLOUR

Grate potatoes and drain. Add beaten egg, salt and enough flour to make a stiff dough. Dip a spoon in water and use it to drop dough into boiling salted water (2 quarts water, 1 teaspoon salt). As soon as dumplings float to the top, they are done. Drain in colander.

Note: 1 1/2 lbs. of spareribs can be substituted for the duck.

Chicken Booyah for a Crowd

"Booyah is a 'soup' that is native to Northeastern Wisconsin. It is served at church picnics, parties–everywhere people get together to have a good time and to share fun and friendship. Historically, booyah is served at 'Kermis' (harvest) time and at fall picnics."

Barbara E. Frisbie—Green Bay

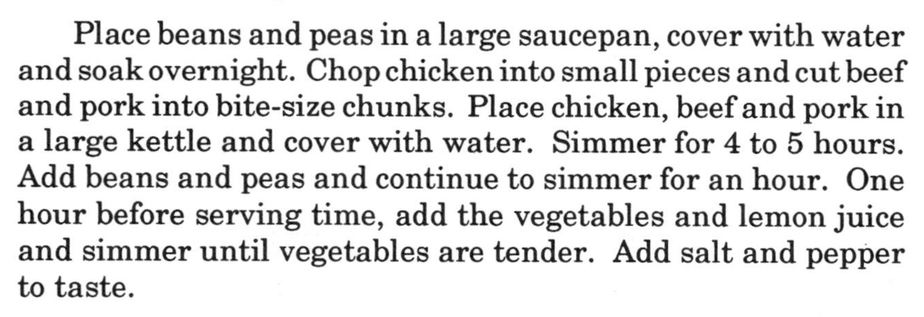

10 qts. dried BEANS
10 qts. dried PEAS
12 STEWING CHICKENS
3 lbs. BEEF
3 lbs. PORK
10 qts. diced CARROTS
20 qts. diced POTATOES
3 sm. heads CABBAGE, chopped
3 qts. diced ONIONS
3 bunches diced CELERY
36 ears of fresh CORN, kernels removed
JUICE of 6 LEMONS
SALT and PEPPER to taste

Place beans and peas in a large saucepan, cover with water and soak overnight. Chop chicken into small pieces and cut beef and pork into bite-size chunks. Place chicken, beef and pork in a large kettle and cover with water. Simmer for 4 to 5 hours. Add beans and peas and continue to simmer for an hour. One hour before serving time, add the vegetables and lemon juice and simmer until vegetables are tender. Add salt and pepper to taste.

Note: "Some cooks add 5 quarts of stewed tomatoes, others a pound of sweet creamery butter. A few bay leaves cooked with the meat add a piquant taste. Add vegetables you like, omit the ones you don't (I add diced rutabagas). Several oxtails are a great substitute for the pork and beef."

Dad's Booyah

"This soup is said to be Belgian in origin. This is a Polish variation."

John Robaidek—Krakow

4 lbs. boned, uncooked CHICKEN, cubed
1 lb. uncooked BEEF, cubed
1 lb. sliced CABBAGE
1 lb. diced CELERY
1 lb. diced CARROTS
1 lb. cubed POTATOES
1 can (15 oz.) CORN, drained
1 can (15 oz.) PEAS, drained
1 can (16 oz.) TOMATOES, undrained
1 1/4 Tbsp. POULTRY SEASONING
1/2 tsp. BLACK PEPPER
1/8 cup SALT
2 cans (15 oz. ea.) CHICKEN BROTH
3-4 CHICKEN BOUILLON CUBES

Place all ingredients in a large kettle, cover with water and simmer until meat and vegetables are tender.

Brunswick Stew

A family favorite on cold winter days.

Cliff Rauscher—Green Bay

5 lbs. RABBIT MEAT
1/4 lb. BUTTER
1 can (10 oz.) condensed TOMATO SOUP
3 TOMATOES, quartered
1 ONION, sliced thin
2 POTATOES, sliced thin
1 cup GREEN LIMA BEANS
SALT and PEPPER to taste
1 cup WHOLE KERNEL CORN
1/4 lb. BUTTER
FLOUR

Cut rabbit meat into 1" cubes. In a skillet, brown meat in butter. Place meat in a large stewing pot; cover with water and boil for one hour. Add tomato soup, tomatoes, onion, potatoes, beans and salt and pepper; cook until vegetables are tender. Add corn and butter and simmer for ten minutes. Combine a small amount of flour and cold water until smooth and add to stew for thickening. Add more seasoning as desired.

Milwaukee Pork Stew

Tammy Vaassen—Wisconsin Pork Producers, Lancaster

2 lbs. boneless PORK SHOULDER or SIRLOIN, cut into 1/2" cubes
1/3 cup ALL-PURPOSE FLOUR
1 1/2 tsp. SALT
1/4 tsp. BLACK PEPPER
2 Tbsp. VEGETABLE OIL
4 lg. ONIONS, cut into 1/2" slices
1 clove GARLIC, minced
1/4 cup chopped fresh PARSLEY
1 tsp. CARAWAY SEED
1 BAY LEAF
1 can (15 oz.) CHICKEN BROTH
1 can (12 oz.) BEER
2 Tbsp. RED WINE VINEGAR
1 Tbsp. (packed) BROWN SUGAR

Dredge pork in combined flour, salt and pepper. Heat oil in a Dutch oven and brown meat over medium-high heat. Add onions and garlic. Cook and stir for 5 minutes. Pour off drippings. Stir in remaining ingredients. Bring to a boil; cover and cook over medium-low heat for 1 to 1 1/4 hours or until meat is very tender. Stir occasionally. Serves 8.

Milwaukee

With its population of over 600,000, Milwaukee is the largest city in Wisconsin, one of its busiest ports and a major grain market. It is also a leading center of German-American culture in the United States. Well-known as a leader in the brewing industry, Milwaukee is among the nation's principal industrial cities and is sometimes called the "machine shop of America." The Menomonee River winds through the city to meet Lake Michigan in Milwaukee Bay.

Sour Cream Soup

"After their Chicago marriage in 1911, my parents, Mary and Joe Dolejs moved to the Bohemian settlement of Ormsby in the town of Peck."

Lorraine Dolejs Fellner—Aniwa

2 med. POTATOES, peeled and cubed
1 1/2 cups WATER
1/2 tsp. SALT
1 1/2 cups WHOLE MILK
1 cup HALF and HALF
1 Tbsp. BUTTER
EGGS (as many as you wish)
1/2 cup SOUR CREAM
1 tsp. dry DILL WEED
2 Tbsp. CIDER VINEGAR

In a saucepan, cook potatoes in salted water until tender. Remove from heat. Add milk, cream and butter and heat on low heat. Crack each egg and place on a saucer; carefully slide them into the potato mixture. When yolks are just firm, remove from soup with a slotted spoon. Add sour cream and dill and simmer to warm (do not boil). Return eggs to pan to heat. Add vinegar and stir. Serve in shallow soup dishes, garnished with fresh dill.

24-Hour Fruit Salad

"This easy-to-prepare salad is delicious and inexpensive."

Delia Brown—Sturgeon Bay

1 can (8 1/4 oz.) PINEAPPLE CHUNKS
1 can (16 oz.) FRUIT COCKTAIL
1 can (11 oz.) MANDARIN ORANGES
1 cup SOUR CREAM
2 Tbsp. POWDERED SUGAR
3 cups MINIATURE MARSHMALLOWS
1 pkg. (3 1/2 oz.) FLAKE COCONUT
LETTUCE

Drain fruit well. Combine sour cream and sugar. In a large fruit bowl, mix together the sour cream, fruit, marshmallows and coconut. Cover and chill in refrigerator for 24 hours. Serve on a bed of lettuce. Serves 8.

Julie's German Potato Salad

"As a new bride, I tried to make a potato salad as good as my husband's German mother had made. After many attempts, I finally succeeded! My highest compliment came when my second generation, Wisconsin German, Mother-in-Law said that my salad was even better than hers!"

Julie Schoessow—Racine

1/2 lb. BACON, diced
3 lbs. sm. RED POTATOES, boiled, peeled and sliced
2 Tbsp. FLOUR
1/3 cup SUGAR
2 tsp. SALT
1/4 tsp. PEPPER
1/4 cup CIDER VINEGAR
1/4 cup LEMON JUICE
1 cup WATER
1 sm. ONION, chopped

In a skillet, fry bacon until crisp. Remove bacon from skillet and drain on paper towels. Pour off all but 1/3 cup of drippings. Combine flour, sugar, salt and pepper in a bowl. Combine vinegar, lemon juice and water in another. Heat bacon drippings until quite hot. Add dry ingredients and, stirring quickly, add liquid mixture and onion. Stir until mixture is smooth and thickened. Pour mixture over potatoes and combine. Serve warm if possible, but definitely at room temperature.

Note: Recipe may be increased by using 5 pounds of potatoes, 1 pound of bacon and doubling the rest of ingredients.

Did you know?

"Gemütlichkeit" is a German word for hospitality or good fellowship.

Wisconsin-Style Maple Bacon Salad Dressing

Wisconsin Dept. of Agriculture—Alice in Dairyland, Madison

8 slices BACON, cut into 1-inch pieces
OLIVE OIL
2/3 cup chopped BERMUDA ONION
1 clove GARLIC, crushed
1/2 cup RED WINE VINEGAR
1/2 cup WISCONSIN MAPLE SYRUP
1/4 tsp. SALT
1 cup MAYONNAISE
2 Tbsp. minced or 1 Tbsp. dried CHIVES

Stir-fry bacon in a large saucepan until extremely crisp. Remove bacon with slotted spoon and drain on paper towels. Pour all of bacon drippings into a glass measuring cup and if necessary, add olive oil to bring the level to 1/2 cup. Return to saucepan. Add onions and garlic and sauté until onions are translucent. Remove pan from heat and pour in vinegar. Add maple syrup. Over low heat, blend mixture with wire whisk and heat until warm. Whisk in salt, mayonnaise and chives until smooth and blended. Remove from heat. This dressing is especially good over spinach or other green salads.

Note: This dressing should be bottled while warm and stored in the refrigerator at all times.

Alice in Dairyland

As a public relations specialist with the Division of Marketing at the Wisconsin Department of Agriculture, Trade & Consumer Protection, "Alice" promotes Wisconsin's agriculture and agri-businesses. She works with news media, addresses rural and urban audiences, conducts food demonstrations, and teaches students about all aspects of Wisconsin agriculture. "Alice" appears at more than 370 events each year including cranberry, apple, cherry, watermelon and maple syrup festivals as well as the Wisconsin State Fair.

Strawberry-Spinach Salad

Marilyn won first place with this recipe!

Marilyn Stephan—Elkhorn
5th Annual Wisconsin Berry Recipe Contest sponsored by the Wisconsin Berry Growers Assn.

1 lb. ASPARAGUS SPEARS
8 cups fresh SPINACH or assorted GREENS
2 cups sliced fresh STRAWBERRIES and BLUEBERRIES
3/4-1 lb. cooked TURKEY, cubed
1/4 cup PECANS

Dressing:
1/2 cup BOTTLED POPPY SEED or ITALIAN DRESSING
1 tsp. grated ORANGE PEEL
1 Tbsp. ORANGE JUICE

Cut asparagus into 1-inch pieces and cook until tender. Drain and rinse with cool water. Let stand in water until cool. Drain. In a salad bowl, combine asparagus, spinach (or greens), berries and turkey. Combine orange peel and orange juice with dressing of choice. Add to salad bowl mixture and toss. Top with pecans. Serves 4.

Super Mystery Salad

"This delightfully surprising salad is elegant enough for any special occasion."

Janie Nelson—Kenosha

3 pkgs. (3 oz. ea.) RASPBERRY GELATIN
1 1/2 cups BOILING WATER
2 cans (16 oz. ea.) crushed TOMATOES, drained
12 drops HOT SAUCE
1 Tsp. HORSERADISH
1 tsp. SUGAR
8 oz. SOUR CREAM

Dissolve gelatin in boiling water. Add tomatoes and gelatin to blender. Blend until smooth; add hot sauce and stir. Pour mixture into molds or serving dish and refrigerate until firm. Combine horseradish, sugar and sour cream for topping.

Cranberry-Kraut Meatballs

"Cranberries and sauerkraut–as 'Wisconsin' as it gets!"

Sally Singstock—Racine

Meatballs:

- 2 lbs. GROUND BEEF
- 1 pkg. ONION SOUP MIX
- 2 EGGS
- 1 cup BREAD CRUMBS

Sauce:

- 1 can (16 oz.) WHOLE CRANBERRY SAUCE
- 1 can (14 oz.) SAUERKRAUT
- 1 cup BROWN SUGAR
- 1 bottle (12 oz.) CHILI SAUCE
- 1 1/2 cups WATER

Mix ground beef with soup mix, eggs and bread crumbs. Form into small meatballs. Place meatballs in a 9 x 12 baking pan. Combine all sauce ingredients in a saucepan and simmer for 15 minutes. Pour sauce over meatballs and bake in 350° oven for 1 hour covered and 1 hour uncovered. Serve with rice or pasta and a salad for a great meal! Meatballs may be frozen. Defrost and heat for easy appetizers or other future use.

Indoor Fish Boil

"This recipe originated with the early commercial fishermen who boiled their fresh catch in buckets on pot-bellied stoves right on the boat. Lake trout are highly prized for both food and sport fishing. The tasty whitefish are native to the Great Lakes."

Ruth Grubbe—The Village Inn, Cornucopia

4 qts. WATER
4 Tbsp. SALT
12 sm. RED POTATOES
10 sm. (1-inch) whole ONIONS, peeled
2 Tbsp. CARAWAY SEEDS
2 Tbsp. DILL SEEDS
2 Tbsp. PEPPERCORNS
3 Tbsp. fresh chopped PARSLEY
3 to 4 lbs. fresh LAKE SUPERIOR WHITEFISH or LAKE TROUT FILLETS, chunked
1 1/2 sticks BUTTER, melted
1 or 2 fresh LEMONS, quartered

Place water and salt in a large kettle, preferably one with a wire basket (a canning kettle works fine). Add potatoes and onions. Place caraway seeds, dill seeds, peppercorns and parsley in a cheesecloth bag. Add to kettle. Boil all for 20 minutes at a steady rolling boil. Drop the fish in and boil for 10 more minutes, or until fish is just done and flakes easily with a fork. Skim off any surface scum. Drain, then ladle on platters with a slotted spoon. Serve immediately with melted butter and fresh lemon. This recipe, along with coleslaw and rye rolls will feed six hungry people.

Cornucopia

"Cornucopia is a small village of less than 200 full-time residents. Our post office is the northern-most post office in the state. In the 40's and 50's there were over 20 commercial fishing boats going out of our harbor. Today we have only one."

Ruth Grubbe

Hungarian-Style Sweet & Sour Pork

"Both of my husband's parents were born in Budapest, Hungary. This recipe reflects their influence on our style of cooking."

Erna S. Stenzel—West Bend

1 1/2 lbs. PORK SHOULDER, cubed
1/2 cup WATER
1 can (20 oz.) PINEAPPLE CHUNKS
1/4 cup BROWN SUGAR
2 Tbsp. CORNSTARCH
1/4 cup VINEGAR
2 to 3 Tbsp. SOY SAUCE
1/2 tsp. SALT
1 RED BELL PEPPER, diced
1/4 cup ONION, diced

In a large skillet, brown the pork in a small amount of cooking oil. Add the water, cover and simmer for 1 hour or until meat is tender. *Do not boil!* Drain the pineapple and reserve the syrup. In a bowl, combine the brown sugar and cornstarch. Add the pineapple syrup, vinegar, soy sauce and salt. Add the brown sugar mixture to the pork. Cook and stir until the gravy thickens. Add the pineapple chunks, bell pepper and onion. Cook for 2 or 3 minutes. Serve over hot rice with a dollop of sour cream. Serves 4 to 6.

Ron's Bear Roast

"Wild game meat is a staple in our diet, but this bear roast is everyone's favorite!"

Ron Wittwer—Grey's Barber Shop, Hayward

1 (4 lb.) BEAR ROAST
1 1/2 cups WATER
1 pkg. LIPTON® ONION SOUP MIX
4 ONIONS, chopped
1 Tbsp. chopped GARLIC
1 bag BABY CARROTS
4 stalks CELERY, diced
6-8 RED POTATOES
1 lb. fresh MUSHROOMS

Place roast in a large roasting pan, add water, soup mix, onions and garlic. Bake at 300° for 2 hours or until meat is tender, adding small amounts of water as necessary. Add vegetables and roast for another hour or until vegetables are done.

Sausage-Kraut Dish

"This German recipe was given to me by a former supervisor who lived in the Fox Valley area for many years."

Judith Fuerbringer—Appleton

6 slices BACON
2 Tbsp. FLOUR
2 jars (16 oz. ea.) MEETERS® SAUERKRAUT
4 lg. RED POTATOES, cut to bite-size pieces
2 MCINTOSH APPLES, cubed
1 ring KIELBASA SAUSAGE, cut into 2-inch pieces
1 tsp. CARAWAY SEEDS
1/2 cup WATER
1 1/2 Tbsp. BROWN SUGAR

Fry bacon until crisp. Remove from skillet with slotted spoon, drain on paper towels and crumble. Add flour to skillet and combine. Add sauerkraut and stir. Place mixture in large bowl, add potatoes, apples, bacon and sausage. Mix well. Add caraway seeds, water and brown sugar and combine all. Place mixture in a 2-quart casserole dish and bake at 350° for 50 minutes to an hour. Serves 4.

Stuffed Meat Loaf

"I created this recipe about 20 years ago. Occasionally I add different ingredients, but I really prefer these."

Laura Pucker—Rosendale

1 1/2-2 lbs. GROUND BEEF
1 sm. jar GREEN OLIVES, cut in half
1 sm. can BUTTON MUSHROOMS
5 slices SWISS CHEESE
5-6 slices HAM
1 can (10.75 oz.) TOMATO SOUP

Form beef into a rectangle shape. Sprinkle olives over the top of the meat. Spread mushrooms on top of the olives and layer cheese. Layer ham over all. Roll meat up (cinnamon roll-style), place in a loaf pan and bake 1 hour at 350°. Pour tomato soup over the top of the meat and bake for another 15 minutes.

Mom's Ragoût of Beef with Dumplings

"This was one of my mother's favorite 'busy day' meals. She would make the ragoût ahead of time and then finish the meal in just 30 minutes at dinner time."

Susan Martin—Portage

Ragoût:

1 1/2 lbs. STEW MEAT, cut into chunks
1 Tbsp. OLIVE OIL (or MARGARINE)
1 med. ONION, diced
1-2 cloves GARLIC, minced
4 cups canned TOMATOES (undrained)
1 tsp. SALT
1 bay leaf
10 WHOLE CLOVES

Brown meat in olive oil. Add onions and garlic and sauté until translucent. Transfer all (including drippings) to a large sauce pan. Add tomatoes and salt. Make a *bouquet garni* with a small piece of cheesecloth tied around the bay leaf and cloves and add to saucepan. Simmer for one hour. Remove the *bouquet garni*. If preparing ahead, cover saucepan and place in refrigerator. Thirty minutes before serving time, bring meat mixture to a simmer and spoon dollops of ***Ragoût Dumpling*** dough on top. Cover and cook for 12-15 minutes. Do not remove cover during this time. Serves 4.

Ragoût Dumplings

1 1/2 cups FLOUR
2 tsp. BAKING POWDER
1/2 tsp. SALT
1 Tbsp. minced PARSLEY
2/3 cup MILK
2 Tbsp. VEGETABLE OIL
1 egg, lightly beaten

Mix together the dry ingredients, and then add the milk, oil and egg, stirring lightly, just until dry ingredients are moistened.

Did you know?

Ragoût, pronounced "ra-GOO", comes from a French word (ragoûter) which means "to stimulate the appetite."

Wisconsin Sauerbraten

"This was my grandmother, Josephine Schaus', recipe."

JoAnn Taylor—Bayside

SALT and PEPPER
4 lbs. CHUCK ROAST
1 lg. ONION, sliced
3 BAY LEAVES
1 tsp. PEPPERCORNS
6 WHOLE CLOVES
1 cup VINEGAR
1 cup WATER
SALT and SUGAR
6 GINGER SNAPS, crushed

Sprinkle meat with salt and pepper and rub in. Place meat in a deep glass or ceramic bowl and add the onion, bay leaves, peppercorns and cloves. Heat vinegar and water, add salt and sugar to taste (sweet and sour). Pour hot liquid over meat to cover and keep covered in refrigerator for at least 4 days (turning twice a day). Place meat in a covered pan with some of the marinade. Brown in hot oven and then bake about 3 hours or until done. Add more vinegar/sugar mixture as needed. Remove meat and set aside. Strain juices and heat in a skillet. Add crushed ginger snaps to thicken. Pour sauce over meat and serve. Sweet and sour red cabbage, dumplings or spätzle are often served with this dish.

Did you know?

The Fox River which runs from its source near Portage and then on into Green Bay, is one of the few rivers in the nation that flows in a northerly direction.

Roast Pheasant with Wild Rice Stuffing

Dorothy Schmitz—Mac Farlane Pheasant Farm, Inc., Janesville

2 PHEASANTS

Remove giblets and reserve for gravy or other use. Rinse birds inside and out and dry thoroughly. Lightly salt and pepper the whole pheasant and stuff loosely with ***Wild Rice Stuffing.*** (Any remaining dressing may be placed around the pheasants or baked in a covered dish alongside the birds.) Tie legs together and turn wings under body. Place breast side up in a shallow roasting pan and brush with melted butter or your favorite basting recipe. Roast at 325° for 30 minutes per pound (plus a total of thirty additional minutes for stuffing), or until tender. If left uncovered, baste frequently. Bacon strips secured over the breast with toothpicks and/or 1 cup of broth (poured over the bird and into the pan) may be added.

Wild Rice Stuffing

1 cup WILD RICE
1 cup thinly sliced ONIONS
1 cup thinly sliced CELERY
1/4 cup BUTTER
2 tsp. PARSLEY (cut fine if fresh)
3 cups day-old BREAD, cut into small cubes
1 tsp. LEAF SAGE (or to taste)
1 1/2 cups CHICKEN STOCK or 1 CHICKEN BOUILLON CUBE dissolved in 1 1/2 cups water

Wash wild rice three times or until rinse water runs clear. Drop into 4 cups of boiling water, cover and simmer for 20 minutes without stirring. Sauté onions and celery in butter until translucent. Add parsley. Place all ingredients in a large bowl and stir to combine.

Kluski Noodle Casserole

"This is my favorite Polish recipe."

Ruth A. Cherveny—Kewaunee

2 lg. PORK STEAKS, cut into small pieces
1 med. ONION
1 lg. pkg. KLUSKI® NOODLES
SALT and PEPPER to taste
2 cans (10.75 oz. ea.) MUSHROOM SOUP
1 can WATER
1-1 1/2 cans (14 oz. ea.) SAUERKRAUT

Brown meat and sauté onion. Cook Kluski noodles according to package directions. Layer the bottom of a buttered casserole dish with 1/2 of steak and onion mixture. Add a layer of 1/2 of the noodles and sprinkle with salt and pepper. Combine soup with water and pour half of the soup mixture over the noodles. Add 1/2 of the sauerkraut. Repeat layers. Bake, covered, at 350° for 1 1/2 hours.

Heidi's Turner Hall Käsekuchen

(Cheese Pie)

"This is a unique and popular Swiss dish that is served at the Monroe Turner Hall, home and headquarters of the Monroe Swiss Singers."

Marian B. Karlen—Monroe

6 EGGS
2 cups CREAM
1 tsp. SALT
1/4 cup grated ONIONS
3 cups grated SWISS CHEESE
1 (9-inch) unbaked PIE SHELL

Preheat oven to 400°. Beat eggs and cream together. Add salt and onion; fold in cheese and pour all into pie shell. Bake at 400° for 10 minutes, then at 350° for 35 minutes. Serve hot, garnished with fresh fruit (the Swiss use grapes).

Baked "Reddened" Wisconsin Trout

"Our trout farm has been in existence since 1856 when Western Wisconsin and the St. Croix River Valley was first homesteaded. We have owned the farm since 1984."

Wisconsin Aquaculture Assn.
Star Prairie Trout Farm, Star Prairie

1/2 cup dried BREAD CRUMBS
1 Tbsp. grated LEMON PEEL
2 tsp. PAPRIKA
2 tsp. dried OREGANO
1/2-1 tsp. dried RED PEPPER FLAKES
1/2 tsp. KOSHER SALT
1/4 cup HALF and HALF
1 EGG
1/4 tsp. SUGAR
6 boneless TROUT FILLETS

Preheat oven to 450°. Lightly grease a baking sheet or line with foil. Mix the bread crumbs, lemon peel, paprika, oregano, salt and red pepper flakes in a shallow baking pan. Lightly beat the half & half, egg and sugar in a small bowl. One at a time, dip the fillets first in the egg mixture and then in the crumb mixture. Arrange fillets on the prepared baking sheet and bake until sizzling and cooked through (12-14 minutes). Serve immediately with ***Lime-Watercress Sauce*** on the side. Serves 6.

Lime-Watercress Sauce

1 EGG YOLK
1 cup minced WATERCRESS LEAVES*
1/4 cup chopped GREEN ONIONS
3-4 Tbsp. fresh LIME JUICE
1 lg. clove GARLIC, crushed
1 Tbsp. DIJON MUSTARD
1/2 tsp. SALT
ground BLACK PEPPER
3/4 cup VEGETABLE OIL (olive or canola)
2 tsp. grated LIME PEEL

Purée egg yolk, watercress, green onion, garlic, lime juice, mustard, salt and pepper (to taste) in a food processor until smooth. While processing, slowly add the oil in a thin stream and continue to process until sauce is thick and smooth. Transfer to a bowl and stir in the grated lime peel. Cover and refrigerate. Serve on the same day prepared due to perishability.

*Parsley or cilantro may be substituted for the watercress.

Alex LeTourneau's Venison Bake

"This recipe came originally from my grandfather Alex who was a Hayward-area resort operator for many years."

Steve Dunster—Camp 4 Deer Camp, Hayward

1/2 cup FLOUR
1/4 tsp. SAGE
1/4 tsp. ROSEMARY
1/4 tsp. BLACK PEPPER
1 tsp. SALT
4 lbs. VENISON TENDERLOIN cut into 1-inch cubes
5 Tbsp. BUTTER
1/2 lb. thin-sliced COOKED HAM cut into 3-inch strips
4 cups diced raw POTATOES
6 ONIONS, thinly sliced
1/2 cup BEEF BOUILLON
1/2 lb. MUSHROOMS, sliced
1/2 cup RED WINE
2 cups SOUR CREAM

Combine flour, sage, rosemary, pepper and salt in a bowl. Dredge venison cubes in mixture until well coated. Melt butter in a large skillet and brown venison well on all sides. Set aside.

Line the bottom and sides of a 2-quart greased casserole dish with the ham slices. Add a layer of 1/3 of the venison, then 1/3 of the potatoes, then 1/3 of the onions. Repeat layers twice. Pour the bouillon over top and bake, covered, at 350° for 45 minutes (add a small amount of water if mixture seems too dry). Distribute mushrooms over top, sprinkle with wine and then spread with the sour cream. Bake an additional 30 minutes or until meat is tender. Serves 8-10.

Hayward
The "Muskie Capital of the World"

Hayward Area Events:

- ***June*** *– Annual Muskie Festival Parade.*
- ***July*** *– The World Championship Lumberjack Events.*
- ***February*** *– Dyno American Birkebeiner Ski Event, North America's largest cross country ski marathon.*

Baked Muskie

"My parents, Frank and Gladys LeTourneau operated the Cedar Lodge resort on Big Spider Lake near Hayward for 53 years. This is my father's muskie recipe."

Irene LeTourneau Regorrah—Cable

1 lg. (9 lb. or better) MUSKIE
SALT and PEPPER

Stuffing*:

chunked STALE BREAD
chopped ONION
coarsely chopped PARSLEY
SALT and PEPPER to taste
canned TOMATO SOUP
canned MILK

Build a fire in a hole that is longer than your fish (including the board), about 2 feet wide and 18 inches deep.

Gut fish and remove scales. Rinse thoroughly. Sprinkle interior with salt and pepper. In a large bowl, combine the stale bread, onion, a generous quantity of parsley and the salt and pepper. Fold in equal amounts of soup and milk (stuffing should be on the wet side). With a large needle and fishing line, sew down the gill covers and stitch together the lips. Stuff fish with stuffing mix and then sew up the the stomach cavity opening.

Wrap fish in four or five layers of dry newspaper, folding paper back from head and tail. Tie entire fish with string (like a rolled roast). Place a dozen or more layers of paper in water and soak until saturated. Wrap fish as before, tying securly with string. Tie the musky to a board that is a few inches larger than it is.

Remove hot coals from your pit and set aside. Place muskie and board in the pit and cover with the coals. Add wood to your fire and keep adding wood and cooking your fish for at least 2 hours (for a 9 lb. fish).

*Stuffing quantities will vary according to the size of your fish.

Hayward Lakes Area

Did you know? *The world's largest muskie (69 lbs. 11 oz.) was taken in the Hayward area in 1949.*

German Salisbury Steak

"I came to America from Germany in 1948 and my mother came in 1951. She was a terrific cook and baker. This is her recipe."

Lillian Marckz—Summit Lake

1 1/2 cans (10.75 oz. ea.) CREAM of MUSHROOM SOUP
2 Tbsp. WORCESTERSHIRE SAUCE
1 Tbsp. DIJON MUSTARD
1 tsp. prepared HORSERADISH
1 EGG
1/4 cup crushed CRACKERS
1/2 cup chopped ONIONS
1/2 tsp. SALT
1/4 tsp. SAGE
1/2 tsp. GARLIC SALT
dash of PEPPER
1 1/2 lbs. lean GROUND BEEF
VEGETABLE OIL
1/2 cup WATER
3 Tbsp. chopped PARSLEY

Combine the soup, Worcestershire sauce, mustard and horseradish in a bowl. Blend well. In another bowl, beat the egg, add cracker crumbs, onions, seasonings and 1/2 cup of the soup mixture. Add meat and mix well. Shape mixture into patties. Place oil in a skillet and brown patties on both sides. Drain. Mix remaining soup mixture with the water and pour over patties. Cover and cook over low heat for 15 minutes or until meat is done. To serve, place patties on a serving plate, spoon sauce over top and sprinkle with the chopped parsley.

Note: I always make a double batch of this recipe because it freezes so well and then I have a quick meal for a busy day.

Superior

Superior is a port on Lake Superior and has one of the largest ore docks in the world. It also has one of the largest grain elevators (13 million bushels) in the United States. Shipbuilding is an important industry here. There are also large flour mills, railroad and machine shops, canneries and breweries. The 4,500-acre Superior Municipal Forest offers 20 miles of trails for skiing and hiking.

Barbecued Ribs German-Style

"As farmers, my family raised its own hogs and butchered them. We used this recipe many times."

Loretta Kochan—Manitowoc

3 lbs. PORK RIBS
1 Tbsp. BUTTER
2 tsp. SALT
1 tsp. PEPPER
1/4 cup VINEGAR
1 can (10.75 oz.) TOMATO SOUP
4 Tbsp. WORCESTERSHIRE SAUCE
4 Tbsp. BROWN SUGAR
1 tsp. MUSTARD
2 tsp. PAPRIKA
1/2 cup CHILI SAUCE
1/4 cup each chopped:
ONIONS,
GREEN BELL PEPPER
CELERY
1 BAY LEAF

Place ribs in a large roasting pan. Combine the remaining ingredients together and pour over the ribs. Cover and bake at 325°, uncovered, for 3 hours. Remove bay leaf before serving.

Grandma's Meat Loaf

"This was a favorite Sunday night supper at my grandmother, Mary Wolf Stoffel's home. Her addition of hard-boiled eggs to the center of the meat loaf always amused us."

Marlene M. Reinders—West Bend

1 1/2 lb. PORK SHOULDER
1 med. ONION
1 1/4 cups dried BREAD CUBES
2 EGGS
1/4 tsp. PEPPER
1 tsp. SALT
1/4 tsp. NUTMEG
3-5 hard cooked EGGS, peeled
CRACKER CRUMBS

Remove excess fat from pork, cut into small chunks and run both the meat and the onion through a food chopper. Soak bread cubes in water, drain and press out water. Add bread, raw eggs and spices to meat mixture. Grease a long, narrow bread pan and sprinkle cracker crumbs on the bottom. Place 1/3 of the meat mixture in pan and position the boiled eggs along the center. Cover with remaining meat mixture. Bake in a 375° oven for about 1 hour. Slice, and serve either hot or cold.

Roast Venison

"This was my Grandmother's favorite recipe."

Cliff Rauscher—Green Bay

5-7 lb. VENISON LEG ROAST
1/4 lb. sliced SALT PORK

Marinade:

1 qt. WATER
1 1/2 cups VINEGAR
2 ONIONS, chopped
1 CARROT, diced
2 cloves GARLIC
1 tsp. dried THYME
4 sprigs PARSLEY
12 PEPPERCORNS
1 Tbsp. SALT
SALAD OIL

Combine marinade ingredients together in a saucepan. Simmer for one hour and then let cool. In a large glass bowl or dish, cover venison with marinade. Allow to marinate at least twenty-four hours in the refrigerator. Preheat a shallow oven pan at 450°. Remove venison from marinade, sprinkle with salt and cover with pork slices. Place meat in preheated pan and add enough salad oil to cover the bottom of the pan. Bake at 450° allowing fifteen minutes per pound for medium-rare and twenty to twenty-five minutes per pound for well-done.

Judd's Shrimp Alfredo

"This original recipe was used by my husband, Mike, during the 5 years he cooked at Judd's Supper Club in Cambridge."

Debra J. Rusch—Lamp Post Inn Bed & Breakfast, Fort Atkinson

4 oz. FETTUCINI
1 1/2 Tbsp. CLARIFIED BUTTER
20 PEA PODS, deveined
1 GREEN ONION, chopped fine
16 lg. SHRIMP
1 cup HEAVY CREAM
dash of GARLIC SALT
1/8 cup ROMANO CHEESE

Cook fettucini according to package directions. Sauté pea pods and onions in clarified butter. When pods are slightly tender, add shrimp, cream and garlic. Continue cooking until cream cooks down to a sauce and shrimp are done. Stir in cheese. Serve shrimp and sauce over fettucini.

Emu Braciole

Doris Donofrie— Shemu Farms, Wausaukee

1 1/2 lbs. TOP LOIN EMU STEAKS
1 Tbsp. OLIVE OIL
2-3 large cloves GARLIC, pressed
4-6 slices BACON, partially cooked and drained
1/3 cup fresh PARSLEY, minced
1/3 cup PARMESAN or SWISS cheese, grated
1/4 tsp. coarsely ground PEPPER
8 oz. HERB SEASONED TOMATO SAUCE

Pound emu steaks with a meat mallet to a thickness of about 1/4-inch, being careful not to tear the meat. Rub olive oil over the surface of the meat and then rub with garlic. Place bacon slices lengthwise on top of the meat. Mix together the parsley, cheese and pepper and sprinkle over meat to within 1/4-inch of the outside edges. Carefully roll the meat, jellyroll fashion, tucking the ends in as you begin the roll. Secure roll with string or toothpicks. Place olive oil in a hot skillet and quickly brown emu roll on all sides. Place rolls in a roasting pan, seam side down and cover with the tomato sauce. Bake, covered, in a 350° oven for 45 minutes. Let sit for 5-10 minutes and then slice into 1 1/2-inch slices. Garnish with parsley and serve with your favorite pasta or fresh green salad. Serves 4-6.

Andrews Drive-In BBQ

"My parents operated the Andrews Drive-In in Fond du Lac in the 1960s. People came from miles away just to savor my mom's special BBQ dish."

Sherrie Wittkopf—Fond du Lac

3 lbs. GROUND BEEF
1 cup chopped CELERY
2/3 cup WATER
1 med. GREEN BELL PEPPER, chopped
2 cans (10.75 oz. ea.) TOMATO SOUP
1 cup KETCHUP
SALT and PEPPER to taste
1 med. ONION, chopped

Brown beef in a large heavy kettle. Drain off drippings and add the balance of ingredients. Cook at 350° for 2-2 1/2 hours, stirring occasionally.

Mother's Rouladen

(Beef Rollups)

"This recipe is typical of the foods served in a German household. It goes back generations beyond my great grandmother. I have adjusted the recipe through the years to suit our tastes."

Gloria A. Warczak—Cedarburg

1 1/2 lbs. lean, boneless ROUND STEAK, 1/4-inch thick
2 Tbsp. VINEGAR, divided
2 Tbsp. low-sodium SOY SAUCE, divided
1/2 tsp. ground BLACK PEPPER, divided
1 strip BACON, cut into 6 pieces
6 pieces diced GREEN BELL PEPPER
6 small pieces ONION
6 small, thin slices SWEET AND SOUR PICKLE
2 Tbsp. VEGETABLE OIL
1 med. ONION, sliced
6 whole MUSHROOMS
3 CARROTS, sliced
2 cloves GARLIC, peeled and crushed
2 Tbsp. chopped PARSLEY
1 cup WATER
1/2 cup BURGUNDY WINE
2 Tbsp. DARK STEAK SAUCE
1 Tbsp. WORCESTERSHIRE SAUCE
1/2 tsp. granulated BEEF BOUILLON
1/4 tsp. dried BASIL LEAVES
1/4 tsp. SUGAR
4 whole PEPPERCORNS
2 WHOLE CLOVES
1 med. BAY LEAF
PARSLEY for garnish

Gravy:
2 Tbsp. CORNSTARCH
1/4 cup WATER

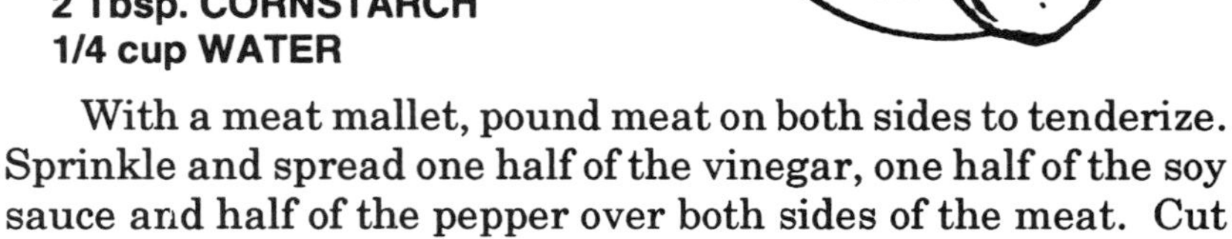
With a meat mallet, pound meat on both sides to tenderize. Sprinkle and spread one half of the vinegar, one half of the soy sauce and half of the pepper over both sides of the meat. Cut

(Continued on next page)

Mother's Rouladen (continued)

steak into 6 pieces. Place one piece each of bacon, green pepper, onion and pickle in the center of each piece of meat. Roll up jelly roll-style and secure with string or toothpicks. Heat oil in a large nonstick skillet. Add rollups and brown slowly on all sides. When meat has browned, add onion, mushrooms, and carrots and cook until onion is translucent. Add garlic and parsley and sauté one minute longer. Add balance of ingredients (except parsley). Bring to a boil, lower heat, cover and simmer for 1 1/2 hours or until meat is tender. Add more water if necessary. Remove rollups and place on a serving platter. To make gravy; heat pan liquids (approximately 1 1/2 cups—add water or water/wine combination if necessary) to almost boiling and gradually stir in the cornstarch which has been mixed with the 1/4 cup water. Stir constantly until mixture thickens. Pour some of the gravy over the meat and garnish with parsley. Serve balance of gravy on the side.

Polish Noodles & Cabbage

(Kluski z Kapusta po Polski)

Mrs. Dolores Haugen—Fond du Lac

1/4 cup BUTTER or MARGARINE
1/2 cup chopped ONION
4 cups chopped (or sliced) CABBAGE
1 tsp. CARAWAY SEED
1/2 tsp. SALT
1/8 tsp. PEPPER
1 pkg. (8 oz.) EGG NOODLES
1/2 cup SOUR CREAM

Melt butter in a large skillet; add onion and sauté until soft. Add cabbage and sauté five minutes or until crisp yet tender. Stir in caraway seed, salt, and pepper. Cook noodles according to package directions and drain well. Stir noodles into cabbage mixture and stir in sour cream. Cook 5 minutes longer, stirring frequently. Serves 6 to 8.

Dairyland Chicken Dinner

"I won the Sauk County dairy bake-off in 1968 with this recipe and went on to win the District contest. The prize was a mink stole!"

Lerna Mae Wiese—Loganville

3/4 cup chopped ONIONS
1/2 cup diced CELERY
1 cup diced CARROTS
1/4 cup CHICKEN BROTH
1 can (10.75 oz.) CREAM of CHICKEN SOUP
1 cup DAIRY SOUR CREAM
3 cups cooked and cubed CHICKEN
1/2 cup sliced MUSHROOMS
1 tsp. SALT
1 tsp. WORCESTERSHIRE SAUCE
1/8 tsp. PEPPER

Combine onions, celery, carrots and chicken broth in a saucepan and simmer for 20 minutes. Place the balance of ingredients in a casserole dish and mix in the vegetables. Top with ***Confetti Topping***. Serves 6-8.

Confetti Topping

1 cup sifted ALL-PURPOSE FLOUR
2 tsp. BAKING POWDER
1/2 tsp. SALT
2 EGGS, slightly beaten
1/2 cup MILK
1 Tbsp. dried or freshly chopped GREEN BELL PEPPER
1 Tbsp. chopped PIMENTO
1 1/4 cups shredded CHEDDAR CHEESE

In a mixing bowl, combine flour, baking powder and salt. Add eggs, milk, bell pepper, pimento and 1 cup of cheese. Mix just until blended. Drop tablespoons of topping onto top of casserole. Bake in a 350° oven for 40-45 minutes or until golden brown. Sprinkle with remaining cheese and bake until cheese begins to melt.

Slavic Sauerkraut Supper

"This recipe was handed down to me by my grandmother who was born in Czechoslovakia. In her day, Grandma made a cream sauce from scratch. I have modernized the recipe by using cream of mushroom soup."

Maree Huber (93 years young)—Fond Du Lac

1 pkg. (8 oz.) NOODLES
1 1/2 lbs. SAUERKRAUT
1 tsp. CARAWAY SEED
1 lb. BEEF STEAK, diced
1 lb. PORK STEAK, diced
1/8 tsp. SALT
1/4 cup chopped ONIONS
1/2 cup diced CELERY
1 can (10.75 oz.) CREAM of MUSHROOM SOUP
1 1/2 cups WATER
1/2 cup BUTTERED BREAD CRUMBS

Cook noodles according to package instructions and then drain. Rinse the sauerkraut and then cook with the caraway seed for 30 minutes. Drain. In a large skillet, brown the meats; season with salt and simmer for 30 minutes. Add onions and celery the last 15 minutes. Combine soup with water and add to the meat mixture. Add the noodles and sauerkraut mixture. Place all in a casserole dish and top with buttered crumbs. Bake at 350° for 45 minutes.

Polish Beans

"My Mother's favorite bean recipe."

Larry Galbraith—Oneida

Cook a batch of **NORTHERN BEANS** and then refrigerate them overnight. When ready to serve, place beans in a skillet with a 4-inch **POLISH SAUSAGE** that has been split down the middle, a small diced **ONION** and **KETCHUP** to taste. Let mixture cook for about an hour before serving.

Pierogi

"Polish pierogi are often served during Lenten season."

Phyllis Reinert— Two Rivers

2 cups FLOUR
2 EGGS
1/2 tsp. SALT
1/4 cup BUTTER

Mix flour, eggs and salt together. Add enough water to make a medium-soft dough. Knead dough until blisters appear. Roll dough thin and cut into 2-inch squares. Place a spoonful of filling (see below) in each. Fold corner to corner to form a triangle. Pinch edges to seal. Drop pierogi into boiling water. When pierogi floats to the top (about 10 minutes), they are done. Melt butter in a skillet and cook until lightly browned. Brush over tops of pierogi.

Cheese Filling: Combine 1/2 lb. dry cottage cheese, 1 beaten egg, 1/8 tsp. salt.

Cabbage or Kraut Filling: 1 head cabbage (1 lb.) chopped fine, 1/2 tsp. salt, 2 Tbsp. butter, 1 med. onion, chopped fine. Sauté onion in butter, add cabbage or kraut, fry slowly until brown.

Potato Filling: Combine 1 large cooked and mashed potato and 1/2 tsp. salt. Add and blend 1/2 cup grated yellow cheese.

Prune Filling: 1/2 lb. prunes, cooked and mashed.

Baked Beans

"This is one of my mom's favorite recipes."

Judy Parins—Green Bay

2 lbs. dry GREAT NORTHERN BEANS
1 med. ONION, diced
1 1/2 Tbsp. SALT
1/2 Tbsp. DRY MUSTARD
4 Tbsp. MOLASSES
4 Tbsp. KETCHUP
1 lb. BACON, lightly fried and drained

Wash beans and place in a 4-quart saucepan. Add water to cover, plus 2 inches. Soak overnight. In the morning, add balance of ingredients and bake for 4 hours in a 325° oven. Uncover for the last hour of baking.

Crock Pot Method: Wash beans and place in a 4-quart crock pot. Add water to cover, plus 2 inches. Add onion and salt and cook on Low overnight. In the morning, add balance of ingredients and cook on High until beans are soft (4-5 hours).

Addie's Zucchini in Creamy Dill Sauce

"I created this recipe in order to have something new to do with the bounty of these prolific vines of summer."

Adeline Halfmann—Arbor Vitae

1/2 tsp. CHICKEN BOUILLON GRANULES
1/3 cup LIGHT SOUR CREAM
2 tsp. OLIVE OIL
1/3 cup coarsely chopped ONION
1 sm. clove GARLIC, minced
2 to 3 sm. ZUCCHINI, quartered lengthwise and cut into 2-inch pieces
1 tsp. dried DILLWEED

In a small bowl or cup, combine bouillon and sour cream; set aside. In a large skillet over medium heat, preheat oil 2 minutes; sauté onions 2 minutes, stirring frequently. Add garlic and zucchini strips; cook and stir just until zucchini is crisp tender. Spoon sour cream mixture over zucchini and sprinkle with dillweed. Toss to coat thoroughly; cook just until heated through (cream will separate if boiled). Serve at once. Serves 4 to 6.

Minocqua, Arbor Vitae and Woodruff Area

Known as the Lakeland Area, this is one of the most beautiful destinations in North America. With over 3200 lakes, streams and ponds, it is recognized as having one of the largest concentrations of freshwater in the world.

Surrounded by the magnificence of the Northern Highlands–the American Legion State Forest–it is a vacationer's paradise summer, winter, spring and fall. Sunup through sundown, the Lakeland area is breathtaking beyond imagination.

Cranberry Ice

"This was my mother's favorite recipe to serve for Thanksgiving and Christmas dinners."

Donna L. Burke—Elm Grove

1 qt. CRANBERRIES
2 cups WATER
2 cups SUGAR
1 ORANGE, juiced and rind finely grated
1 tsp. GELATIN

Wash cranberries and remove stems. Place cranberries and water in a saucepan and cook until they are soft and the skins pop open. Strain and then mash the cranberries through a sieve back into the saucepan. Squeeze juice from orange into a bowl, add the gelatin and allow to dissolve; add to cranberry mixture. Add orange rind and sugar. Heat mixture until the sugar is dissolved. Cool and freeze. When mixture is frozen, remove and beat until light. Freeze again until ready to serve.

Potato Dumplings

"My Bohemian/Polish grandmother (Mary Noskowiak) often served this dish with her sauerkraut and pork dinners."

Mary Jo (Noskowiak) Stefanescu—Racine

8 lg. POTATOES
1 EGG
1/2 tsp. BAKING POWDER
FLOUR
1/2 lb. BACON, chopped
1 lg. ONION, chopped
SALT and PEPPER to taste

Grate potatoes and remove excess moisture. Mix egg and then baking powder into the grated potatoes. Gradually add in enough flour to make a stiff, but slightly sticky dough. Fill a large saucepan with water (add a dash of salt) and heat on high heat. When hot, drop potato mixture from a teaspoon into water. Cook and occasionally stir lightly. When dumplings float to the top, remove and set aside to drain. Brown bacon in a large skillet. When well browned, add the onions and cook until onions are also brown. Add dumplings to bacon mixture with salt and pepper to taste. Mix well, cover and allow to cook about 20 minutes over medium heat, stirring occasionally.

Fried Cabbage

"My grandmother used to make this in the fall when cabbage from the garden was plentiful."

Jeanine Jacobs—Antigo

8 slices BACON
6 cups shredded CABBAGE
2 1/2 cups thinly sliced CELERY
1 lg. GREEN BELL PEPPER, cut into thin strips
2 med. ONIONS, sliced thin then quartered
1/4 cup SUGAR
SALT and PEPPER to taste

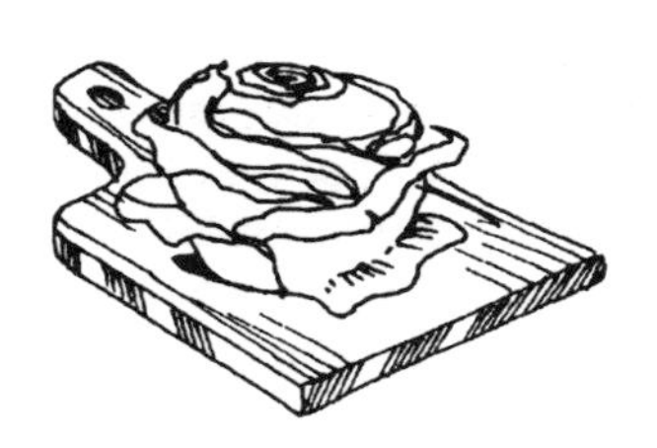

In a 6-quart kettle, fry bacon until crisp. Remove and set aside. Combine balance of ingredients (in the order given) with the bacon drippings in kettle. Cover and cook over medium to low heat for about 15 minutes. Stir, and continue to cook slowly for another 25 minutes. Place cabbage mixture in a serving bowl and top with crumbled bacon. Serves 6.

Roesti

(Swiss Fried Potatoes)

Marian B. Karlen—Monroe

4 Tbsp. BUTTER
1 ONION, chopped
6-8 boiled POTATOES*, peeled and shredded
1/2 cup shredded SWISS CHEESE

Melt butter in skillet; add onion and sauté until translucent. Add potatoes and cheese; stir just to combine. Fry (without stirring) for 5 to 10 minutes or until a golden crust has formed on the bottom. Turn, press potatoes down and brown the other side.

*Potatoes should be boiled the day before they are shredded.

Rutayama Whip

"Rutabagas were on sale . . . but how to get the grandchildren to eat them? They loved my holiday yams . . . thus was born this healthy, tasty side dish."

Susan Martin—Portage

2 lg. RUTABAGAS, peeled and diced into 1-inch cubes
2 lbs. YAMS, peeled and cut into chunks
1 stick (8 Tbsp.) MARGARINE
3/4 cup chopped ONION
3/4 cup dry, unseasoned BREAD CRUMBS
3 EGGS, beaten
2 Tbsp. BROWN or WHITE SUGAR
SALT and PEPPER to taste

Place rutabagas in a large saucepan and cover generously with water. Cover and boil, over medium-high heat, for 30 minutes. Add yams to the saucepan and boil an additional 30 minutes. Drain rutabagas and yams thoroughly, using a large colander. Add the margarine to the same saucepan and return the rutabagas and yams to the pan. Add the chopped onion. With an electric mixer, beat the vegetables until the margarine has melted and the rutabagas and yams are the consistency of creamy mashed potatoes. (The mixture will be lumpy, however, because of the onions.) Fold in the bread crumbs. Mix together the eggs, sugar, salt and pepper; add to the vegetables and whip all until thoroughly mixed. Pour into a lightly greased 2-quart baking dish*. Bake, uncovered, in a 350° oven for 40-45 minutes. If desired, buttered bread crumbs may be put on the top for the last 10 minutes of baking. Serves 6 to 8.

*This dish may be prepared ahead of time and refrigerated, covered, for up to one day. Add an additional 15 minutes to baking time.

Did you know?

Rutabaga—the name of this cabbage-family root vegetable comes from the Swedish "rotabagge". It is sometimes called a Swedish turnip or simply a Swede.

Honey Cranberry Relish

"This recipe was invented by 'Grandma' Diehnelt. It is served at many family meals and get-togethers."

Walter Diehnelt—Honey Acres, Inc., Ashippun

2 cups fresh CRANBERRIES, stems removed
2 cored APPLES
2 whole ORANGES, halved and seeded
1 cup HONEY

Run cranberries, apples and oranges (including peelings) through a food processor. Add honey, mix well, and refrigerate overnight.

Waupaca

Waupaca is a popular departure point for canoe and launch trips. In the winter, groomed trails throughout Waupaca County offer snowmobilers an excellent opportunity to test their riding and driving skills.

Beet Pickles

"This is my mother's recipe. I take these pickles to our senior citizens center dinners–they love them because they can no longer do their own canning."

Lois Dorschner—Waupaca

2 qts. cooked BEETS, cubed

Sauce:

2 cups VINEGAR
2 cups WATER
2 cups SUGAR
1 tsp. CLOVES
1 tsp. CINNAMON
1 tsp. ALLSPICE

Combine sauce ingredients in a saucepan and bring to a boil. Pour over beets in sterilized glass jars, and seal according to manufacturer's directions.

Sweet Chunk Pickles

"This is a favorite of our family. The recipe was handed down from my aunt, Mrs. Earl (Irene) Evans."

Janice Evans Swanek—Neenah

2 gal. CUCUMBERS, chunked (about 1" x 1")
2 cups CANNING SALT
1 gal. WATER
2 Tbsp. powdered ALUM

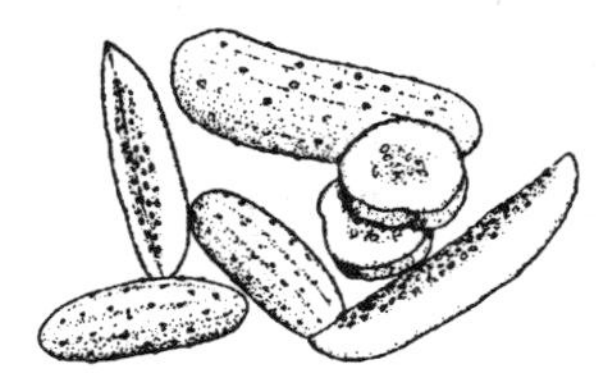

Brine:

6 pts. (12 cups) SUGAR
5 cups VINEGAR
1 Tbsp. CELERY SEED
1 Tbsp. mixed PICKLING SPICE
5 sticks CINNAMON

Boil water, add salt and stir until salt is dissolved. Place cucumber chunks in a 4-5 gallon crock (or use glass or glazed container–do not use metal). Add saltwater to cover and weigh down with a heavy plate to keep chunks submerged. Let sit for 1 week, skimming off any mold that may develop.

Drain and discard liquid. Rinse container well. Return cucumbers to crock and cover with 1 gallon boiling water. Weigh down with a plate and let stand for 48 hours. Drain. In a saucepan, add alum to 1 gallon of water, boil and then pour over pickles. Let stand for 48 hours. Drain. Combine brine ingredients in a saucepan and bring to a boil. Pour over pickles. Reheat liquid daily for 4 days. Drain (reserving brine). Pack pickles into sterilized pint jars, filling jars tightly. Heat reserved brine and pour into pickle jars to fill. Seal with canning lids and rings according to manufacturers directions.

Note: It takes 2 weeks to make these pickles, but they are well worth the effort.

MUFFINS, ROLLS & BREADS

Wisconsin Apple-Cranberry Muffins

"This is a favorite at our house."

Sheila Zahorik—Eau Claire

1 1/2 cups FLOUR
3 tsp. BAKING POWDER
1 tsp. CINNAMON
1 cup OLD-FASHIONED ROLLED OATS
1/2 cup firmly packed BROWN SUGAR
1/4 cup BUTTER, melted
1 cup MILK
1/4 cup SOUR CREAM
2 EGGS
1 cup peeled, chopped APPLES
1/2 cup halved CRANBERRIES
2 Tbsp. SUGAR

Preheat oven to 425°. Butter 18 muffin cups. In a large bowl, combine flour, baking powder, and cinnamon. Mix well. Stir in oats and brown sugar. In a medium bowl, beat together the butter, milk, sour cream and eggs until well blended. Add to dry ingredients. Mix until moist. Stir in apples and cranberries. Fill muffin cups 3/4 full and sprinkle sugar evenly over tops. Bake for 15-20 minutes or until light golden brown.

3-Day Rolls

(aka "Kupper Buns")

"I have made these buns for years as has my daughter-in-law who lives in Florida. My late husband Gene Kupper was always proud to deliver the buns to whomever I had made them for. We laughed because I would tell him, 'Go deliver my buns!'"

Nancy Kupper Hartfield—Racine

1 lg. pkg. CAKE YEAST or 3 pkgs. DRY YEAST
2 cups SUGAR
4 cups WARM WATER
3 EGGS
1 Tbsp. SALT
1 cup CORN OIL
12-13 cups FLOUR

First Evening: In a bowl, mix together yeast, 1 cup sugar and 1 cup warm water. Cover and set aside.

The Following Morning: In a large bowl, mix together the second cup of sugar, eggs, salt and corn oil. Add 3 cups warm water, the yeast mixture and enough flour to make a soft dough. Place in a large greased bowl and cover. Punch dough down as it rises throughout the day.

At Bedtime: Shape dough into buns and place on a greased cookie sheet. Cover with a towel and let rise overnight.

The Next Morning: Bake buns in a 350° oven for 10-12 minutes. Makes 60-84 buns, depending upon size.

Racine

Situated just south of Milwaukee, this city occupies a promontory jutting into Lake Michigan and is bisected by the Root River. Like most Wisconsin cities, Racine is multinational in makeup, but the emphasis is Danish. Of special interest–the Frank Lloyd Wright-designed administration building of the Johnson Wax Company. A theatre housed here presents screenings of award-winning films.

American Ginseng Banana Muffins

"In Chinese, the word 'ginseng' is directly translated as 'the essence of man'. For over two thousand years, ginseng has been used in the Orient as a whole body tonic to support the five visceral organs, calm the nerves, tranquilize the mind, clear the eyes, and improve the memory. Cultivation of American ginseng began in the 1880s."

Kim Kohlbeck—Hsu's Ginseng Enterprises, Inc., Wausau

3 AMERICAN GINSENG TEA BAGS or,
2 Tbsp. AMERICAN GINSENG POWDER
3 Tbsp. HOT WATER
2 soft med. BANANAS
2 EGGS
1/2 cup SUGAR
1 Tbsp. OIL
1/2 tsp. CINNAMON
1/2 tsp. BAKING SODA
1 1/2 cups FLOUR
1/8 tsp. SALT

Allow contents of 3 tea bags (or ginseng powder) to soak in 3 tablespoons hot water for 15 minutes. Mix bananas, eggs, sugar, oil and ginseng (and water) until well blended. Sift together dry ingredients and add to banana mixture and mix well. Pour into 12 greased muffin cups and bake at 350° for approximately 15 minutes.

Wausau

Wausau has come a long way from the sawmill settlement called Big Bull Falls. This busy industrial center is the county seat of Marathon County which is one of the nation's leading producers of cheddar cheese and American ginseng.

Date Crumb Muffins

"This was my mother's recipe from the 1930's. It's great for variety, and reheats nicely."

Donna L. Burke—Elm Grove

1/4 cup SHORTENING
1/4 cup SUGAR
1 EGG, well-beaten
1 cup sifted FLOUR
4 tsp. BAKING POWDER
1/2 tsp. SALT
1 cup fine dry BREAD CRUMBS
1 cup MILK
1/2 cup chopped DATES

Cream shortening and sugar together until fluffy. Stir in egg. Sift flour with baking powder and salt, add crumbs and then add to shortening mixture alternating with milk. Stir in dates. Fill well-greased muffin tins and bake at 350° for 25 to 30 minutes.

Apple-Date Cornbread

"My mother, who was born in Brighton, England used to make this cornbread during the depression."

Joy M. Baye—Green Bay

2 cups YELLOW CORNMEAL
1/2 cup BROWN SUGAR
1 tsp. SALT
1 3/4 cups MILK
2 Tbsp. BUTTER
2 EGGS, beaten
2 tsp. BAKING POWDER
1 cup peeled and diced APPLES
1/2 cup chopped DATES
1/2 tsp. NUTMEG

Combine cornmeal, brown sugar, salt, milk and butter in the top of a double boiler. Cook and stir mixture over boiling hot water until thick. Cool slightly. Add eggs and baking powder to cornmeal mixture. Mix thoroughly. Stir in apples and dates. Pour mixture into a greased square baking pan and sprinkle top with nutmeg. Bake for 35 minutes at 375°.

Chocolate Chip Banana Bread

"Burlington is known as 'Chocolate City', so I try to serve chocolate in muffins, cookies, and breads for each breakfast at our Inn. When a guest suggested adding chocolate chips to banana bread, I revised my recipe and added coconut too."

Gayle Hohner—The Hillcrest Inn and Carriage House, Burlington

1/2 cup BUTTER
1 cup SUGAR
2 EGGS
1 tsp. VANILLA
3 mashed BANANAS
1/2 cup SOUR CREAM
1 1/2 cups FLOUR
1 tsp. BAKING SODA
1/2 tsp. SALT
1/2 cup chopped NUTS
1/2 cup shredded COCONUT
1 cup CHOCOLATE CHIPS

Cream butter and sugar together. Add eggs, vanilla, bananas, and sour cream. Mix well. Combine flour, baking soda and salt and stir into sugar mixture. Stir in nuts, coconut and chips. Pour into a greased 9 x 5 loaf pan and bake at 350° for 1 hour.

Zucchini Bread

"This bread is the next thing to a Holiday Fruit Cake. Aging enhances the flavor, it freezes well, and has luscious nutrients."

Delia Brown—Sturgeon Bay

3 cups FLOUR
2 tsp. BAKING SODA
1 tsp. SALT
1/4 tsp. BAKING POWDER
1 1/2 tsp. CINNAMON
1/2 tsp. NUTMEG
3 EGGS
1 cup OIL
2 cups SUGAR
2 tsp. VANILLA
2 cups shredded ZUCCHINI
1 can (8 oz.) crushed PINEAPPLE, drained
1 cup chopped NUTS
1 cup RAISINS, CURRANTS or DATES

In a large bowl, combine flour, soda, salt, baking powder and spices. In another bowl, beat the eggs, oil, sugar and vanilla until thick. Stir in zucchini, pineapple and flour mixture. Mix well. Fold in fruits and nuts. Pour mixture into 2 (5 x 9) loaf pans. Bake for 1 hour in a 325° oven. Test for doneness.

Whole-Wheat Bran Bread

"This bread is great toasted! My family especially likes it made into grilled cheese sandwiches."

Lucille Welton—Washburn

1/2 cup BULGAR WHEAT
1 cup BOILING WATER
1 cup WATER
3/4 cup MILK
3 Tbsp. HONEY
4 tsp. SALT
6 Tbsp. CRISCO®
1/3 cup MOLASSES
1/2 cup WARM WATER
2 pkgs. YEAST
1 cup BRAN
3 cups WHOLE-WHEAT FLOUR
2 1/2 to 3 cups WHITE FLOUR

Place bulgar wheat in a bowl and add 1 cup boiling water. Allow mixture to stand until water is absorbed (10-20 minutes). In a saucepan, combine 1 cup water and milk and heat to boiling. Stir in soaked bulgar, honey, salt, Crisco and molasses. Cool to lukewarm. Place 1/2 cup warm water in a cup and allow yeast to dissolve. Add to bulgar mixture. Add bran and whole-wheat flour to bulgar mixture and beat until smooth. Add enough white flour to form a stiff dough. Knead. Place dough in a greased bowl, grease top, cover and let rise about 1 hour. Punch down and divide into 2 loaves. Place loaves in greased loaf pans, cover and let rise until double (about 1 hour). Bake at 375° for 15 minutes, lower temperature to 350° and bake for an additional 25 minutes.

Bara Brith

(Bread)

"This is a Welsh recipe for bread that my mother used to make. Her parents came to America just 3 years before she was born. There are still several settlements of Welsh in Wisconsin."

Maxine M. Rasmussen—Sturgeon Bay

1 1/2 cups RAISINS
1/4 cup WATER
1/3 cup SHORTENING
2 cups SCALDED MILK
1/3 cup SUGAR
2 tsp. SALT
1 tsp. CINNAMON
1/2 tsp. ALLSPICE
1/2 tsp. CLOVES
1 cake or 1 pkg. YEAST
1/4 cup WARM WATER
5 1/2 to 6 cups FLOUR

Cook raisins in water until puffed and set aside. Add shortening to scalded milk, stir until melted, then add sugar, salt, and spices. Pour milk mixture into a large bowl and stir to lukewarm. Dissolve yeast in 1/4 cup warm water. Add yeast and about 1/2 cup flour to milk mixture. Cover and let rise for 30-50 minutes in a warm place. Add raisins and enough flour to mixture to allow kneading. Continue adding flour and kneading for 8-10 minutes. Place in a greased bowl and let rise until doubled (about 1 hour). Punch down and divide into two rounded pieces. Let rest for 20 minutes. Form into loaves, place in greased bread pans and let rise until tops are well-rounded. Bake for 45-50 minutes in a 350° oven. Cover tops with foil if they become too brown.

Sturgeon Bay

Located about halfway up the Door Peninsula, Sturgeon Bay is one of the largest shipbuilding ports on the Great Lakes. The canal that bisects the peninsula here allows giant freighters, as well as smaller boats, easy access to the Great Lakes from Green Bay. The fruits of approximately 3,000 acres of cherry trees in the surrounding areas are processed here.

Boston Brown Bread

"Due to the fast pace of our lives today, I have created several microwave recipes. This is one that always makes a hit!"

Cheryl J. Wittgreve—Rolling Meadows Sorghum Mill, Elkhart Lake

1/2 cup WHOLE-WHEAT FLOUR
1/4 cup FLOUR
1/4 cup CORNMEAL
1/2 tsp. BAKING POWDER
1/4 tsp. BAKING SODA
1/4 tsp. SALT
1 EGG, beaten
1/4 cup SORGHUM
2 Tbsp. SUGAR
2 tsp. OIL
3/4 cup BUTTERMILK
1/4 cup RAISINS

Combine flours, cornmeal, baking powder, soda and salt. Combine eggs, sorghum, sugar and oil. Add dry ingredients alternately to egg mixture with buttermilk; beat well. Stir in raisins. Spoon batter into four 8-ounce paper drinking cups. Cook in microwave, uncovered, on HIGH for 2 minutes. Rearrange cups, cook 2 1/2 minutes more.

Cranberry-Zucchini Bread

"Cranberries are native to Wisconsin and were one of the state's first exports."

Peggy Anderson—Cranberry Expo Ltd., Warrens

3 EGGS, beaten
2 cups SUGAR
2 cups grated ZUCCHINI
1 cup OIL
2 tsp. VANILLA
2 cups FLOUR
1 tsp. SALT
2 tsp. BAKING SODA
2 tsp. CINNAMON
1 cup halved CRANBERRIES

Combine ingredients; place in 2 regular loaf pans or 4 smaller pans and bake at 350° for 45-60 minutes. Check for doneness with toothpick inserted in center.

Sunny Millet Bread

Natural Ovens of Manitowoc was founded in 1976 by Paul Stitt. Paul and his wife, Barbara, say, "Our mission is to make the best tasting and most nutritious breads possible to help you have vibrant good health".

Barbara Stitt—Natural Ovens of Manitowoc Wisconsin, Manitowoc

2 Tbsp. OIL
2 Tbsp. HONEY
2 1/2 cups WATER
1 cake YEAST
1/4 cup SUNFLOWER SEEDS
1/2 cup CRACKED WHEAT
1 cup WHOLE WHEAT FLOUR
2 cups GLUTEN FLOUR
2 cups ROLLED OATS
2 tsp. SALT
1 tsp. BARLEY MALT
3 tsp. SESAME SEEDS
1/4 cup MILLET

Mix all ingredients at once. Knead for 10 minutes (should be slightly sticky). Cover with a board and let rise for 1 hour. Punch down, wait 15 minutes, then form into 2 loaves. Knead to work out all possible air. Allow to double (not higher than half an inch below the top of a regular loaf pan). Bake in greased loaf pans at 350° for about 30 minutes.

Happiness Bread

Also by Natural Ovens, this bread is often served as a dessert!

1/4 cup HONEY
3 Tbsp. OIL
2 oz. cake YEAST
3 1/4 cups WATER
2 1/2 cups WHOLE WHEAT FLOUR
2 1/2 cups GLUTEN FLOUR
1 tsp. MALT
1 Tbsp. POTATO FLOUR
1 cup ROLLED OATS
1/2 tsp. SALT
2 Tbsp. PECAN PIECES
1 tsp. CINNAMON
1 cup RAISINS

Mix all ingredients (except pecan pieces, cinnamon and raisins) together for 12 minutes. Fold in nuts, cinnamon and raisins. Mixture should be slightly sticky. Let rise for one hour. Punch down and let rest for 15 minutes. Knead. Divide into two loaves and place in lightly greased loaf pans. Let double in size. Bake for 30-40 minutes in a 350° oven.

Kolache Dough & Fillings

This recipe, by Marie Machacek, is included courtesy of the Wisconsin Czechs, Inc. and taken from their excellent cookbook Dobré Chutnání. Frances Goetz contributed the following Kolache Filling recipes to that same book.

Sally Teresinski—Wisconsin Czechs, Inc., Oshkosh

3 Tbsp. (level) YEAST
1/2 cup WATER
8 EGG YOLKS
3 tsp. SALT
1 cup SUGAR
1 cup LARD
1 cup MASHED POTATOES
1 can EVAPORATED MILK and enough WATER to make 3 cups
10 cups FLOUR

Dissolve yeast in water. Add some flour to thicken and let set until it bubbles. Cream eggs, salt, sugar and lard. Add potatoes and milk mixture. Stir. Add yeast to the batter. Add flour and stir again. Let rise until double. Punch down. Let rise again. Shape into balls. Let rise and then fill (with fillings of choice–see below). Let rise a few minutes more. Bake at 400° until brown (about 10-12 minutes).

Cheese Filling

2 cups POT or FARMER CHEESE
1/4 cup softened BUTTER
1/4 cup SUGAR
2 EGGS, separated
1/4 cup chopped blanched ALMONDS
1 tsp. grated LEMON RIND
1/4 cup seedless RAISINS

Force cheese through food strainer. Cream butter and sugar and beat in egg yolks. Add almonds, lemon rind and raisins to butter mixture and fold in stiffly beaten egg whites.

Prune Filling

1 lb. dried PRUNES
1/2 cup SUGAR
1 Tbsp. LEMON JUICE
1 tsp. LEMON RIND
1/2 tsp. CINNAMON

Cover prunes with water and cook until soft. Reserving liquids, remove and pit the prunes. Add prunes and sugar to prune liquid and cook over slow heat, stirring constantly, until smooth and thick. Add lemon juice, lemon rind and cinnamon.

Maple Syrup Cake

"We still tap maple trees and boil the sap for maple syrup. Our pantry is always stocked with quarts of syrup for the long winters."

Susan Kolpack—Antigo

1/2 cup BUTTER
1/4 cup SUGAR
3/4 cup MAPLE SYRUP
2 EGGS, beaten
2 1/4 cups FLOUR
2 1/2 tsp. BAKING POWDER
2/3 tsp. BAKING SODA
1/2 tsp. GINGER
1/2 tsp. SALT
1/2 cup MILK

Cream butter and sugar together. Add syrup and eggs. Sift flour, baking powder, baking soda, ginger and salt together. Add dry ingredients alternately with milk to the butter mixture. Bake at 350° for 35-40 minutes. When cool, spread with ***Maple Icing.***

Maple Icing

1 cup MAPLE SYRUP
2 EGG WHITES, stiffly beaten

Boil maple syrup until it spins a thin thread. Add slowly to egg whites and beat until stiff enough to spread over cake.

Walnut Povitica

"My mother came to the U.S. from Croatia in 1904 and she brought this recipe with her. It was baked for her family of fourteen children on every family or holiday occasion."

Catherine M. Delfield—Ashland

2 cups MILK
1/2 cup BUTTER
1/2 cup SUGAR
1 lg. cake YEAST
6 cups FLOUR
4 EGG YOLKS
3 tsp. SALT

Scald milk; add butter and sugar and cool. Dissolve yeast in warm water (about 1/8 cup). Add to milk mixture. Add 3 cups flour and beat well. Add egg yolks and salt. Add rest of flour and knead until smooth and pliable. Cover and let rise in a warm place. When double in size, shake down and let rise again. Roll out as thin as possible on a floured cloth. Spread with ***Walnut Filling.*** Roll jelly roll-style and seal ends. Place in a well-greased pan and cover with cloth. Let rise about 15 minutes. Bake in a 300° oven for 1 hour. Do not remove from pan until cool.

Walnut Filling

1 1/2 lbs. ground WALNUTS
1 1/2 cups HALF and HALF
1 cup BROWN SUGAR
1/2 cup GRANULATED SUGAR
1/2 cup HONEY
3 tsp. CINNAMON
4 Tbsp. BUTTER
2 EGGS

Combine all ingredients (except eggs) in a saucepan. Bring to a boil, mix well and then cool slightly. Add eggs and beat.

Peanut Butter-Honey Cookies

This recipe from the "Every ① A Winner", Blue Ribbon Recipe Cookbook written by Sue-Ann Dondlinger.

Sue-Ann K. Dondlinger—Richfield

1/2 cup MARGARINE
1 cup HONEY
1/2 cup PEANUT BUTTER
1 EGG
1 1/4 cups FLOUR
1/2 tsp. BAKING SODA
1/2 tsp. SALT

Beat margarine and add honey in a fine stream. Beat in peanut butter and egg. Continue beating until fluffy. Stir in dry ingredients. Drop by heaping teaspoonfuls 2 inches apart onto greased cookie sheet. Bake in a 325° oven for 10-12 minutes or until nicely browned. Makes 2 1/2 to 3 dozen cookies.

Prune Whip

"I am 90-years-old, and still enjoy baking and cooking. This recipe is from my collection of old family recipes."

Bernice Griese—Green Bay

1 lb. PRUNES, cooked, pitted and chopped
2 Tbsp. SUGAR
3 EGG WHITES, beaten until stiff

Fold sugar and prunes into egg whites and pour into a baking pan. Bake for 15-20 minutes at 325°. Serve, topped with ***Custard Sauce.***

Custard Sauce

3 EGG YOLKS
2 Tbsp. FLOUR
1/4 cup SUGAR
pinch of SALT
1 tsp. VANILLA
2 cups SCALDED MILK

In the top of a double boiler, beat egg yolks slightly, then stir in flour, sugar, salt and vanilla, alternating with hot scalded milk. Cook and stir until mixture is thick and a coating forms on the spoon.

Cherry-Berry on a Cloud

"This was a 2nd place winner in the dessert category of the 7th Annual Wisconsin Berry Recipe Contest which was sponsored by the Wisconsin Berry Growers Association. This is a state favorite! You will find this recipe in many 'local' cookbooks."

Barb Winkler—Random Lake

Meringue:
- **6 EGG WHITES**
- **1/2 tsp. CREAM OF TARTAR**
- **1/4 tsp. SALT**
- **1 3/4 cups SUGAR**

Filling:
- **2 pkgs. (3 oz. ea.) CREAM CHEESE, softened**
- **1 cup SUGAR**
- **1 tsp. VANILLA**
- **2 cups WHIPPING CREAM, partially whipped and chilled**
- **2 cups MINIATURE MARSHMALLOWS**

Topping:
- **1 can CHERRY PIE FILLING**
- **1 tsp. LEMON JUICE**
- **2 cups fresh STRAWBERRIES (or 1 pkg. frozen)**

Beat egg whites, cream of tartar, and salt until frothy. Gradually beat in sugar and beat until stiff and glossy (about 15 minutes). Spread in a greased 9 x 13 pan and bake at 275° for 60 minutes. Turn off oven and leave meringue in oven overnight or for 12 hours. Oven door MUST remain closed for the entire time to prevent any bacteria from contaminating the meringue. Combine cream cheese, sugar and vanilla and chill. Combine chilled cream cheese mixture with chilled whipping cream and beat until thick. Add marshmallows and spread over top of meringue. Refrigerate for 4 hours or until set. Combine berry topping ingredients and spread over all. Refrigerate again until ready to use.

Grandmother's Apple Crisp

"My grandmother was born, raised and lived in Wisconsin until her death at the age of 94. I have lived in Wisconsin all of my 62 years. Grandmother shared this recipe with me in 1956. It is easy to make and a wonderful delight to eat."

Sally Blair—Hudson

6 to 8 small APPLES, peeled and cored
1/4 cup WATER
1 1/2 tsp. ground CINNAMON
Pinch of SALT

Topping:
1 cup SUGAR
3/4 cup ALL-PURPOSE FLOUR
1/3 cup BUTTER

Preheat oven to 350°. Butter a 9-inch pie plate. Cut apples into 1/2-inch slices and place in pie plate. Pour water over apples and sprinkle with half of the cinnamon and a small pinch of salt. To make the topping; using a pastry blender, mix together sugar, flour, butter and remaining cinnamon until butter is cut to the size of small peas. Sprinkle mixture over apples and, using your hands, pat down lightly. Place pie plate on a foil-lined baking sheet. Bake for 45 to 50 minutes, until apples are tender and top is nicely browned. Serve warm with whipped cream or ice cream.

Taffy Cookies

"Grandma's cookie tin is always full of these!"

Susan Kolpack—Antigo

1 cup BROWN SUGAR
1 cup BUTTER
1 cup chopped PECANS
GRAHAM CRACKERS, crumbled

Place sugar, butter and pecans in a saucepan and boil for 2 minutes. Line a greased cookie sheet with graham cracker crumbs; pour sugar mixture over all and bake for 10 minutes at 350°. Remove from pan immediately, break into cookies and place on wax paper until cool.

Polish Chrusciki

"This recipe is very popular in all communities. It is sometimes also known as 'bow knots'."

Lillian Golonka—Sobieski

12 EGG YOLKS
1 whole EGG
3 Tbsp. SUGAR
6 oz. RUM
4 cups FLOUR
OIL for deep fat frying
POWDERED SUGAR

Beat eggs well, add sugar and beat again. Add rum and then gradually add well-sifted flour to mixture, beating continuously. Knead dough on a floured surface for one-half hour, hitting dough against the board from time to time. Separate dough into four parts. Cover three with waxed paper to keep from drying. One at a time, roll each part very thin (as if for noodles), cut diagonally to strips one inch wide and four or five inches long. Slit each strip lengthwise down the center. Pull one end though the slit to form a knot. Stretch each one slightly. Drop into medium-hot oil, four or five at a time. Submerge each knot with a fork. When golden brown, turn and then remove and drain on paper towels. Sprinkle with powdered sugar.

Danish Crumb Cake

"My Danish mother often made this cake as I was growing up."

Jean Gehrt—Racine

2 cups BROWN SUGAR
1/2 cup SHORTENING
2 cups FLOUR
pinch of SALT
2 Tbsp. CINNAMON
1 cup SOUR MILK
1 tsp. BAKING SODA
2 EGGS

Cream sugar and shortening together. Stir in flour, salt and cinnamon. Reserve 1 cupful of mixture for topping. Add sour milk, baking soda and eggs to sugar mixture. Mix well and then pour into a greased 11 x 7 baking pan. Sprinkle top with reserved topping and, if desired, chopped nuts and chocolate chips. Bake at 325° for 35 minutes, or until center tests done.

Raspberry Dumplings

"This recipe came from a cookbook my grandmother put together. The recipes in her book range in age from the 1920s to the late 1930s."

Nancy Roberts—Green Bay

Batter:

1 cup FLOUR
2 tsp. BAKING POWDER
1/4 tsp. SALT
1/2 cup MILK
1 EGG

Sauce:

2 cups RASPBERRIES
1 cup WATER
1 cup SUGAR

Combine batter ingredients in a medium size bowl. Place sauce ingredients in a saucepan and bring to the boiling point. When the sugar has dissolved, drop batter from a teaspoon into the sauce. Cover and steam until done. Serve with the sauce or with cream on the side.

Rhubarb Dessert

"This was my grandmother's recipe."

Kathy Kuderer—Down A Country Road Bed & Breakfast, Cashton

Crust:

1 cup FLOUR
1/2 cup BUTTER
5 Tbsp. POWDERED SUGAR

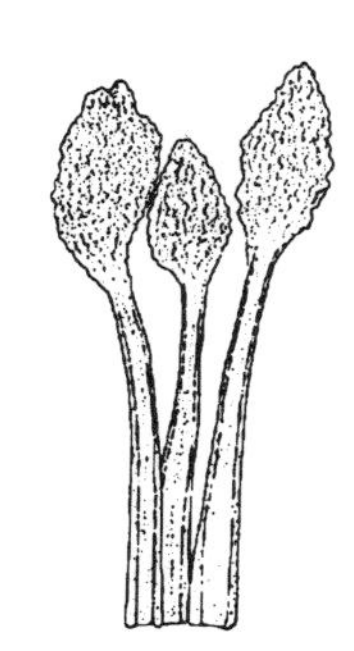

Topping:

1 1/2 cups SUGAR
2 EGGS, beaten
1/4 cup FLOUR
3/4 tsp. SALT
2 cups chopped RHUBARB

Add crust ingredients to a medium-sized bowl and, using a pastry blender, blend to the size of small peas. Press mixture into an ungreased 7 1/2 x 11 baking pan and bake for 15 minutes at 350°. Combine topping ingredients and pour into crust. Bake for 35 minutes at 350°.

Wisconsin Cherry-Apple Crisp

"Apples from Gays Mills, La Crescent, and Eau Claire areas (to name a few), cherries from Door County–you can't get more Wisconsin than this!"

Mrs. Sheila Zahorik—Eau Claire

10 cups peeled and sliced MCINTOSH APPLES
2 cups frozen SWEET CHERRIES, thawed and drained
2 cups OLD-FASHIONED ROLLED OATS
1 cup firmly packed BROWN SUGAR
2/3 cup FLOUR
2/3 cup BUTTER, softened
2 tsp. CINNAMON
1 tsp. NUTMEG

Arrange apples and cherries in a buttered 13 x 9 baking dish. In a medium bowl, combine balance of ingredients and then sprinkle over the apples and cherries. Bake in a preheated 375° oven for 30 to 35 minutes, or until apples are tender. Serve warm.

Strawberry Ice Cream Topping

"My mother made this topping during the strawberry harvest so that we would have it all year long."

Margie Dustin—Viroqua

2 qts. STRAWBERRIES
6 cups SUGAR, divided

Scald berries in boiling water for 2 minutes and then drain. Add 4 cups sugar and boil for 2 minutes, counting time after entire contents of saucepan is bubbling. Remove from heat. When the bubbling stops, add 2 more cups of sugar. Boil 5 minutes longer, counting time as before. Pour mixture into shallow pans so topping is not over 1 1/2 to 2 inches deep. Let stand overnight. Pack in small jars and freeze.

Sunday Special Torte

"Several years ago, my Sunday Special Torte recipe won first place in a bake-off contest in our county and then went on to a Madison television contest. I did not win first place there (the prize was a mink stole), but was nevertheless pleased to be an entrant at that level."

Phyllis Schenck—Reedsburg

1 cup (2 sticks) BUTTER
1/2 cup SUGAR
5 EGG YOLKS
2 Tbsp. MILK
1 tsp. VANILLA
1/2 tsp. BAKING POWDER
1/2 tsp. SALT
2 cups ALL-PURPOSE FLOUR, sifted
1 cup RASPBERRY PRESERVES
5 EGG WHITES
1/4 tsp. SALT
1 cup SUGAR
1 1/3 cups flaked COCONUT
1 tsp. VANILLA
2 cups DAIRY SOUR CREAM

Cream butter, gradually adding 1/2 cup sugar and beat until light and fluffy. Blend in egg yolks, milk, vanilla, baking powder and 1/2 teaspoon salt. Beat well. Stir in flour. Spread batter in 3 (round) 9" cake pans which have been buttered on the bottom only. Spread 1/3 cup preserves on each layer to within 1 inch of edges. Beat egg whites and 1/4 teaspoon salt until soft mounds may be formed. Gradually beat in 1 cup sugar, beating until stiff peaks form. Fold in coconut and 1 teaspoon vanilla. Spread over preserves in baking pans. Bake for 35 to 40 minutes in a preheated 350° oven. Cool in pans on wire racks for 15 minutes; remove from pans and cool completely. Spread sour cream between layers leaving the top plain. Chill several hours or overnight.

Note: Any preserve may be used in this recipe; such as strawberry, blueberry or peach.

Pfeffernüesse

(A German Christmas cookie)

"In German, 'pfeffernuesse' means 'peppernuts'. My brother thought of dipping the cookies in the icing to save time when making a large batch."

Susanne Eisen—Oshkosh

4 EGGS
2 cups SUGAR
1/4 tsp. ORANGE FLAVORING
4 oz. CITRON (run through a meat grinder)
4 cups ALL-PURPOSE FLOUR
2 tsp. CINNAMON
1/4 tsp. CLOVES
1/4 tsp. GINGER
1/2 tsp. ALLSPICE
1/2 tsp. PEPPER

Cream eggs and sugar together until creamy and light in color. Stir in orange flavoring and citron. Sift together the flour and spices. Blend egg and flour mixtures. Knead dough. Shape into small balls (smaller than *small* walnuts). Place on greased cookie sheet. Bake at 300° for 15-20 minutes. Cool to warm, then dip in a lemon icing made of **LEMON JUICE** and **SUGAR** (thick, flowing consistency). Drain cookies on rack and store in a closed container after icing has dried.

Pecan Fingers

"When I was a child, my grandmother, Betty Vesperman, made these cookies at Christmastime."

Samantha Buergi—
Green Bay Area Visitor and Convention Bureau, Green Bay

1 cup BUTTER
1/4 cup BROWN SUGAR
2 cups FLOUR
1/2 tsp. SALT
1 Tbsp. WATER
1 tsp. VANILLA
2 cups chopped PECANS
POWDERED SUGAR

Cream butter and sugar well. Add flour, salt, water and vanilla. Stir in pecans and beat. Roll dough out into finger size rolls and cut into 3-inch lengths. Bake at 350° for 18-20 minutes. While still warm, roll cookies in powdered sugar.

Kringla

(A Norwegian Cookie)

Jan Etnier—Eau Claire

2 cups SUGAR
1/2 cup SHORTENING
6 EGG YOLKS
2 tsp. VANILLA
1 cup EVAPORATED MILK
1 cup BUTTERMILK
6 cups FLOUR
2 tsp. BAKING SODA
2 tsp. BAKING POWDER
1/2 tsp. SALT

Cream sugar and shortening together. Add egg yolks and vanilla. Add evaporated milk, buttermilk and dry ingredients and beat until smooth. Chill the dough for 1 hour or more to make it easier to roll. Working with small portions of dough at a time, roll out on a floured cloth to width of a pencil and about 6 inches long. Form dough into figure eights and place on a greased cookie sheet. Bake at 450° for approximately 6 minutes.

Note: Add 1 teaspoon vinegar to 1 cup milk and let stand for 15-30 minutes as a substitute for buttermilk.

Römmegröt

(A Norwegian Cream Pudding)

"This recipe was brought from the 'old country' (as my mother would say) and was a basic dish served in Norwegian homes."

Edna M. Bjorgo—Gilmanton

1 qt. SWEET CREAM
1 cup FLOUR
2 1/2 cups scalded MILK
1/2 tsp. SALT
3-4 Tbsp. SUGAR
CINNAMON

In a saucepan, bring cream to a boil, and stir constantly for about 5 minutes. Sift flour into mixture slowly continuing to stir. Remove butterfat from top when it rises and reserve. Add scalded milk and beat well until mixture is velvety. Let simmer. Add salt and sugar. Remove from saucepan and put in a large bowl. Put reserved butterfat on top and sprinkle with sugar and cinnamon. Serve warm.

Nodji's Cranberry Tassies

"Cranberries are Wisconsin's number one fruit crop and Wisconsin ranks first in the nation for cranberry production."

Nodji Van Wychen—Warrens

Crust:
- **1 pkg. (3 oz.) CREAM CHEESE, softened**
- **1/2 cup BUTTER**
- **1 cup sifted FLOUR**

Filling:
- **1 EGG**
- **3/4 cup packed BROWN SUGAR**
- **1 Tbsp. BUTTER**
- **1 tsp. VANILLA**
- **dash of SALT**
- **2/3 cup coarsely broken PECANS**
- **1 cup quartered fresh CRANBERRIES**

Cream cheese and butter until well blended. Stir in flour until dough forms; chill for 1 hour. Shape dough into 1-inch balls; mold into ungreased miniature muffin tins so that dough covers the bottom and comes up the sides of each. Beat egg, sugar, butter, vanilla and salt until creamy. Divide nuts evenly between muffin cups and then layer with the cranberries. Fill each cup with egg mixture to just fill cups. Bake at 325° for 25 minutes or until filling is set. Makes 2 dozen tassies.

Christmas Dessert

"This is my mother's recipe and a family favorite!"

Florence Roepke—Houlton

- **1 pint WHIPPING CREAM**
- **1/2 tsp. VANILLA**
- **2 tsp. SUGAR**
- **1 cup crushed PEANUTS**
- **2 1/2 cups bite-size pieces APPLE, peeled or unpeeled**

Whip cream and add vanilla and sugar; fold in peanuts. Serve apples in bowls with a dollop of whipped cream mixture on top.

Sour Cream Sugar Cookies

"The first place I always headed for at my Norwegian grandmother's house was the cookie jar–the next was to my grandma for a big hug."

Bonnie Young—Soldiers Grove

1 3/4 cups SUGAR
1 cup BUTTER, softened
3/4 tsp. SALT
4 EGG YOLKS
2 WHOLE EGGS
1 tsp. BAKING SODA
2 Tbsp. HOT WATER
1 cup SOUR CREAM
4 cups FLOUR
1 tsp. BAKING POWDER
SUGAR

Cream sugar, butter, salt, egg yolks and whole eggs. Dissolve baking soda in hot water and add with the sour cream to the sugar mixture. Add and mix the flour and baking powder. Cover and chill for several hours. Roll out dough and cut into large cookies. Sprinkle tops with sugar and bake at 350° for 8-10 minutes or until cookies are set.

Buttermilk Cookies

"These cookies were made by Belgian immigrants to take with them to the fields for a lunch that included milk and cheese. The recipe was given to me by my grandmother."

Kandice S. Bretl—Brussels

3 cups SUGAR
2 cups SHORTENING
4 EGGS, beaten
2 cups BUTTERMILK
2 Tbsp. VANILLA
2 tsp. SALT
3 Tbsp. BAKING POWDER
3 Tbsp. BAKING SODA
5 cups FLOUR

Cream sugar and shortening. Add eggs, buttermilk and vanilla. Sift in salt, baking powder and baking soda. Slowly sift in enough flour to make a soft, pliable dough. Chill at least one hour. Roll dough out and cut out cookies with a large cookie or biscuit cutter. Bake at 350° for about 15 minutes, or until edges just turn a golden brown.

Old-Fashioned Sugar Cookies

"My mother, Ruth Evans, used this recipe to make cut-out cookies for every holiday. The large quantity of cookies that this recipe makes reflects the speed at which they disappeared with six kids in the house."

Janice Evans Swanek—Neenah

11 1/4 cups unsifted FLOUR
2 Tbsp. BAKING SODA
2 tsp. CREAM OF TARTAR
2 tsp. SALT
4 cups SUGAR
3 cups MARGARINE, softened
8 EGGS
1 cup MILK
2 Tbsp. + 2 tsp. VANILLA

In a large bowl, sift together the first five ingredients. Cut in margarine until mixture resembles a coarse meal. Blend in eggs, milk and vanilla. Roll dough out on a lightly floured board to 1/16" thickness and cut into desired shapes. Bake cookies on an ungreased cookie sheet at 400° for 6-8 minutes.

Gudbrandsdal

(Gold Band)

"This recipe was first made by my grandmother in Tynset, Norway before she came to the U.S. in the late 1800s."

Borghild Ramseth Nissen—Green Bay

1 cup SUGAR
1 cup BUTTER or MARGARINE
1 cup CORNSTARCH
2 cups FLOUR
1 cup WHIPPING CREAM
1 tsp. ALMOND FLAVORING
1 cup slivered ALMONDS

Cream sugar and shortening. Add the rest of ingredients to sugar mixture, blending after each addition. Drop from a tablespoon onto greased cookie sheet. Bake at 250° for about 1 1/2 hours, or until light brown around the edges (gold band). Note: This is a no egg, no baking powder recipe. It is very important to bake the cookies long and slow.

Oh So Good Cherry Pie

"Door County is famous for its wonderful sour cherry crops. Many families plan a special day to go 'cherry picking' at one of the many orchards. When I pack cherries for freezing, I measure exactly two cups of cherries and one cup of juice per container, especially for this pie."

Betty Gellings—Eden

Pie shells (3)

1 cup LARD
3 cups FLOUR
1 tsp. SALT
1/3 cup ICE COLD WATER

Cut lard into flour and salt with a pastry blender until mixture is crumbly. Stir in ice water, mixing with a fork until dough is pliable. Divide dough into thirds. Roll out each portion and place in 9 or 10-inch pie pans (metal is best). Wrap and freeze extra pie shells for future use. Flute edges of pie shell and bake for 15 minutes at 350°.

Filling:

1 cup SUGAR
3 Tbsp. CORNSTARCH
1 cup CHERRY JUICE
2 cups pitted SOUR CHERRIES
2-3 drops ALMOND flavoring
2-3 drops RED FOOD COLORING

Mix sugar and cornstarch together in a saucepan. Add cherry juice and stir until well blended. Fold in cherries. Cook over medium heat, stirring constantly, until mixture thickens. Stir in almond flavoring and red food coloring. Pour filling into pie shell.

Topping:

1/2 cup quick-cooking OATMEAL
1/2 cup BROWN SUGAR
4 Tbsp. ALL-PURPOSE FLOUR
4 Tbsp. COLD BUTTER

With a pastry blender, cut oatmeal, brown sugar and flour into butter until mixture is crumbly. Sprinkle over top of cherry filling.

Bake pie for 20 minutes at 350°. Serve warm with a scoop of ice cream; or cold, with a dollop of whipped topping.

Festive Cran-Apple Pie

"In the fall, when fresh apples and cranberries are harvested all across our state, this pie can often be found on our family's table."

Germaine Schommer—Eden

2 cups fresh CRANBERRIES
1 cup SUGAR
1 Tbsp. CORNSTARCH
2 Tbsp. WATER
5-6 cups peeled, sliced APPLES
1/2 cup SUGAR
3 level Tbsp. CORNSTARCH
1/2 tsp. CINNAMON
1/4 tsp. NUTMEG
2 (9-inch) PIE CRUSTS
SUGAR (I use red-colored)

In a saucepan, combine cranberries, 1 cup sugar, 1 tablespoon cornstarch and water. Bring mixture to a boil and boil for 5 minutes. Cool for 15 minutes. In a large bowl, combine apples, sugar, 3 tablespoons of cornstarch, cinnamon and nutmeg. Toss until apple slices are well-coated. Stir in cranberry mixture. Spoon all into pie shell and top with the second pie crust. Vent top with tines of a fork, seal and flute edges. Sprinkle sugar over the top. Bake at 400° for 15 minutes, then at 350° for 35 minutes. Cover edge of pie crust with strips of foil after first 15 minutes of baking to prevent excessive browning.

Schaum Torte

"In German, 'schaum' means 'foam'. This recipe was handed down through generations from my great grandmother. I have continued that tradition by giving it to my granddaughter."

Erma S. Stenzel—West Bend

6 EGG WHITES
2 cups SUGAR
1 tsp. VANILLA
1 tsp. VINEGAR

Beat egg whites until stiff enough to form peaks. Beat in sugar, two tablespoons at a time, 3 times, beating thoroughly after each addition. Beat in vanilla and vinegar and then fold in the remaining sugar. Pour mixture into a greased 10-inch pie pan (or a springform pan) and bake for 1 hour in a 275° oven until firm. Leave torte in oven with the door open until cold. Serve, topped with whipped cream and strawberries.

S'More Pie

"I created this pie several years ago for my children."

Deborah Paulaha—Hudson

Crust:

1 3/4 cups crumbled GRAHAM CRACKERS
1 cup SUGAR
1/2 cup BUTTER, melted

Filling:

2 Tbsp. BUTTER
5 oz. MARSHMALLOWS
4 oz. CREAM CHEESE, whipped
1 tsp. VANILLA
1 pkg. (3.9 oz.) INSTANT CHOCOLATE PUDDING
2 cups MILK

Mix crumbled graham crackers and sugar in a bowl. Add butter and mix thoroughly. Reserve two tablespoons of mixture to decorate top of pie. Press remaining mixture firmly and evenly against bottom and sides of a 10-inch pie pan. In a saucepan, melt the 2 tablespoons butter. Add marshmallows and heat and stir until melted. Add whipped cream cheese and marshmallow mixture to a bowl and blend. Whisk the chocolate pudding mix, milk and vanilla together following package directions. Add to the marshmallow mixture, beating well. Pour into graham cracker crust and decorate with reserved crumbs. Refrigerate overnight.

Swedish Apple Pie

Violet Meyer—Pelican Lake

5-6 peeled, sliced APPLES
1 Tbsp. SUGAR
1 tsp. CINNAMON
1 EGG, beaten
1 cup SUGAR
1 cup FLOUR
1/4 tsp. SALT
1/2 cup chopped NUTS
3/4 cup MARGARINE, melted

Fill a 9-inch pie pan about 3/4 full of apples. Sprinkle top with 1 tablespoon sugar and the cinnamon. In a bowl, combine balance of ingredients. Spread egg mixture over top of apples and bake for 35-45 minutes at 350°.

Kickapoo Orchard Cherry Pie

"We have grown sour cherries in our orchard for many years. This recipe changed many times before it became as it is today. We sell this pie in our bakery."

M. Marlene Meyer—Kickapoo Orchard, Gays Mills

4 cups pitted SOUR CHERRIES
1/4 cup quick-cooking TAPIOCA
1 1/4 cups SUGAR
1/4 tsp. natural ALMOND EXTRACT
2 (9-inch) unbaked PIE CRUSTS

Mix cherries, tapioca, sugar, and almond extract and let stand for at least 15 minutes. Pour filling into pie crust and moisten edges with water. Cover with second crust; pierce the top with tines of a fork to vent. Press fork tines on edges of pie to seal and bake at 400° for 30-40 minutes. Cool before cutting. Serve, topped with vanilla ice cream.

Laverne's Belgian Cheesecake

Laverne Muck—Green Bay

Crust:

2 Tbsp. BUTTER
8 Tbsp. SUGAR
2 EGGS
2 cups FLOUR
2 tsp. BAKING POWDER

Filling:

1 lb. COTTAGE CHEESE
1 cup MILK
1 Tbsp. CORNSTARCH
2 Tbsp. BUTTER
1 cup SUGAR
3 EGGS
1 tsp. VANILLA
pinch of SALT

For crust; blend butter and sugar. Add eggs, then dry ingredients. Mix well. Press and pat mixture onto bottom and sides of 2 oiled pie tins. Mix all filling ingredients together in a blender until smooth. Pour into pie shells and bake at 375° until set (approximately 35-40 minutes).

Alden Caldwell's Pound Cake

"When Alden Gates Caldwell was 11 months old, he and his parents survived the sinking of the Titanic (April 15, 1912). The hand-written recipe for this cake was found in his cottage on the shores of nearby Lac Courte Oreilles. Alden died in 1993. I would like to dedicate this recipe to my one-time friend and neighbor."

Shirley A. Shannon—Stone Lake

2 1/2 cups SUGAR
1/4 lb. MARGARINE
1 cup CRISCO®
1/4 tsp. SALT
1 tsp. VANILLA
6 EGGS
3 tsp. BAKING POWDER
3 cups sifted CAKE FLOUR
3/4 cup MILK

Mix with electric mixer on low speed for 20 minutes. Pour batter into a greased angel food cake pan and bake at 350° for 1 1/4 hours. Frost with ***Pound Cake Frosting.***

Pound Cake Frosting

3/4 stick MARGARINE, melted
dash of SALT
1 EGG WHITE
1 tsp. VANILLA or ALMOND

Beat all ingredients together until light and fluffy.

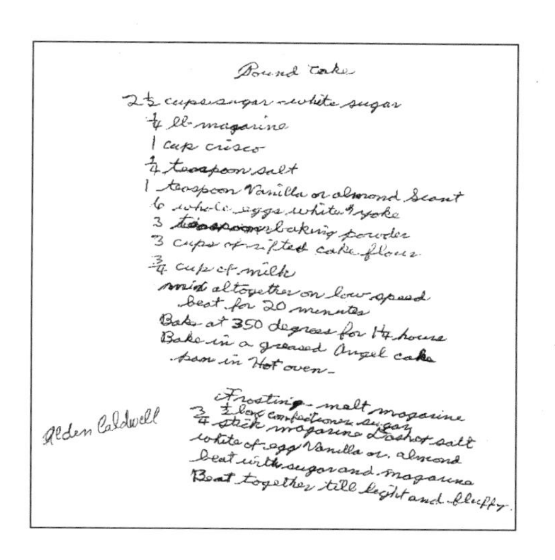

Pound cake

2 1/2 cups sugar white sugar
1/4 lb margarine
1 cup crisco
1/4 teaspoon salt
1 teaspoon Vanilla or almond Scant
6 whole eggs white & yoke
3 ~~teaspoon~~ baking powder
3 cups of sifted cake flour
3/4 cup of milk
mix altogether on low speed
beat for 20 minutes
Bake at 350 degrees for 1 1/4 hours
Bake in a greased Angel cake
pan in Hot oven-

Frosting - melt magarine
3/4 stick magarine Dash of salt
1/2 box confectioner sugar
white of egg Vanilla or almond
beat with sugar and magarine
Beat together till light and fluffy.

Alden Caldwell

Alvina's Belgian Cheesecake

"I've made many cheesecakes, but this is the best one yet!"

Alvina Wagner—St. Nazianz

1 cup COLD WATER
1/2 cup SUGAR
1 1/2 pkgs. unflavored GELATIN
4 EGGS, separated
1/2 cup COLD WATER
1 pkg. (12 oz.) CREAM CHEESE
2 1/2 Tbsp. LEMON JUICE
1 cup WHIPPING CREAM
1 (9-inch) GRAHAM CRACKER PIE CRUST

Place 1 cup cold water, sugar and gelatin in the top of a double boiler. Heat until gelatin dissolves. Beat the egg yolks and 1/2 cup water with an egg beater and add to mixture in double boiler. Stir until mixture thickens (about 8 minutes). Combine the cream cheese and lemon juice and beat until smooth. Stir into the double boiler ingredients. Pour batter into a bowl and refrigerate until thick. Whip the cream and fold into the batter. Beat the egg whites until stiff and fold into the batter. Pour batter into graham cracker crust and refrigerate for 3 to 4 hours.

Orange Date Cake

"This is one of my mom's favorite recipes."

Dolores A. Haugen—Fond du Lac

3/4 cup SHORTENING
1 3/4 cups SUGAR, divided
2 EGGS, beaten
2 1/2 cups FLOUR
1 tsp. BAKING POWDER
1 cup BUTTERMILK
1 tsp. BAKING SODA
1 cup chopped NUTS
1 1/2 cups chopped DATES
juice of 2 ORANGES

Cream shortening and 1 cup sugar together. Add eggs and mix well. Sift together the flour and baking powder. Combine buttermilk and baking soda. Add flour mixture to egg mixture, alternating with buttermilk. Fold in nuts and dates. Bake in a greased tube pan for 45 minutes at 350°. Dissolve 3/4 cup sugar in orange juice. While cake is still hot, poke holes in the top with a fork and pour orange juice over surface. Let cool for 10 minutes before removing cake from pan. Serve with whipped cream or topping.

Rhubarb Refresher

"I would like to share a 'taste of Spring' with you for your book. We especially enjoy this recipe when the rhubarb comes fresh from our garden."

Betty L. Conart—Land's End Employee, Dodgeville

4 cups chopped RHUBARB
2 cups FRUIT JUICE (cranberry, apple, or your choice)
1 cup WHITE SUGAR
1 pkg. (3 oz.) RED, FRUIT-FLAVORED JELLO®

In a saucepan, cover rhubarb with fruit juice and cook until tender. Mash rhubarb and add sugar and jello, stir and let cool. Serve with dollops of ***Rhubarb Topping*** on top.

Rhubarb Topping

1 pint WHIPPING CREAM
1/2 cup BROWN SUGAR
1/2 tsp. MAPLE FLAVORING

Whip all ingredients together and chill until ready to serve.

My Mother's Special Devil's Food Cake

"This recipe came from my grandfather's aunt who got it from, as the title says, her mother!"

Bonnie Denis—Green Bay

1/2 cup SHORTENING
3 cups DARK BROWN SUGAR
2 EGGS, beaten
2 SQUARES COOKING CHOCOLATE, melted
2 1/2 cups sifted CAKE FLOUR
1/4 tsp. SALT
1/2 cup BUTTER
1/2 tsp. VANILLA
1 tsp. BAKING SODA
1 cup BOILING WATER

Cream shortening and brown sugar together. Add eggs, chocolate, flour, salt, butter and vanilla. Mix baking soda in boiling water and add to cake mixture. Pour batter into baking pans and bake in a 350° oven for 40-45 minutes.

Grandma's Dried Apple Cake

"My grandmother-in-law brought this recipe from Virginia. She had it memorized. One day I measured the ingredients as she put them out so that I would have a written version. Be sure to read the recipe through before starting!"

Pauline Goldman—Washburn

Filling:
- **3 cups DRIED APPLES**
- **3 cups WATER**
- **1/2 cup SUGAR**
- **1 1/2 tsp. ALLSPICE**

Dough:
- **1/3 cup SHORTENING**
- **1/2 cup SUGAR**
- **2 EGGS**
- **1/4 cup MOLASSES**
- **1/4 cup BUTTERMILK**
- **3 cups FLOUR**
- **1 tsp. GINGER**
- **1 tsp. BAKING SODA**
- **1/2 tsp. BAKING POWDER**
- **1/4 tsp. SALT**

Combine apples and water in a saucepan, bring to a boil and then let apples soak for 4 hours. Mash apples and then stir in sugar and allspice. Set aside.

Cream together the shortening and sugar. Add eggs, molasses and buttermilk. Sift remaining ingredients together and add to the sugar mixture. Knead dough on a floured board until semi-stiff. Divide dough into 4 pieces and roll each out to about the size of a 9-inch pie pan. Use a plate to trim edges smooth. Place cakes on cookie sheet(s) lined with pastry paper and bake in a 475° oven for about 5 minutes, or until light brown. While still hot, place one cake on a platter, top with a cup of apple mixture and repeat with the balance of layers. Cool and wrap tightly. Refrigerate 5 days before serving.

Hot Milk Cake

"In the 1950's, my father owned the Tracey Corner Cheese Factory in the Bonduel-Cecil area. We lived upstairs above the factory. I remember my mother, Agnes Zehren, serving this cake as a dessert for the family dinner on many occasions."

Catherine Zehren Mueller—De Pere

1 1/2 cups CAKE FLOUR
1 1/2 tsp. BAKING POWDER
pinch of SALT
1 1/2 Tbsp. BUTTER
2/3 cup HOT MILK
3 EGGS, well beaten
1 1/2 cups SUGAR
1 tsp. VANILLA

Combine cake flour with baking powder and salt. Melt butter in the hot milk. Beat flour mixture into eggs, add sugar and beat in the milk. Stir in vanilla. Pour batter into 2 round cake pans and bake for 40-50 minutes at 350°. When done, place cake layer on serving platter, layer with ***Marshmallow-Pineapple Frosting.*** Add second layer and frost all.

Marshmallow-Pineapple Frosting

1 Tbsp. LEMON JUICE
1/3 cup PINEAPPLE JUICE
1 pkg. (10 oz.) MARSHMALLOWS (quartered)
1 cup HEAVY CREAM

Combine lemon and pineapple juices, add quartered marshmallows and let soak for 3-4 hours. Whip cream until stiff and fold in marshmallows.

Manitowoc

Manitowoc has been an important port since the early 1800s, but the multi-million dollar luxury yachts being built here now are a far cry from the schooners and submarines of the past. Cook's Corner, an outlet for much of the aluminumware made in the area (Mirro, Wearever, etc.) is the largest gourmet food and kitchen gadget store in the United States. The Manitowoc-Ludington, Michigan car ferry crosses Lake Michigan daily and saves the long drive north or south to circumvent this gigantic body of water.

Küchen

"This recipe was given to me by my German grandmother."

Mary C. Beau—Green Bay

Crust:

1 tsp. SUGAR
1 cake YEAST
1/4 cup WARM WATER
2 Tbsp. SUGAR
1/2 Tbsp. SALT
1/4 cup SHORTENING
1/4 cup MILK, boiled and cooled
1 EGG
2 cups FLOUR

Add 1 teaspoon sugar and yeast to warm water and let sit until yeast dissolves. Cream 2 tablespoons sugar, salt and shortening together; add yeast mixture and stir in milk, egg and flour. Cover and let rise until double in size. Pat dough out into bottom and sides of an 11 x 15 cake pan.

2 cups sliced APPLES
3/4 cup SUGAR
1/4 cup BUTTER
1/2 tsp. CINNAMON

Layer apples over crust. Cream sugar, butter and cinnamon together and dot over surface of apples.

Topping:

1 cup SUGAR
3/4 cup FLOUR
1 tsp. VANILLA
1/3 cup BUTTER

Cream sugar, flour, vanilla and butter together. Sprinkle over surface of apples. Bake for 35 minutes in a 375° oven.

1/2 cup CREAM
1 tsp. SUGAR
1/2 tsp. VANILLA

Combine cream, sugar and vanilla and pour over top of Küchen. Return to oven for 5 minutes.

Tomato Soup Cake

"This cake is heavy, but very good!"

Judy Parins—Green Bay

1/2 cup BUTTER or SHORTENING
1 cup SUGAR
1 EGG
1 tsp. BAKING SODA
1 can (10.75 oz.) TOMATO SOUP
1/4 cup WATER
1 2/3 cups FLOUR
1 tsp. BAKING POWDER
1 tsp. CINNAMON
1/2 tsp. CLOVES
1/2 tsp. NUTMEG
1/4 tsp. SALT
1 cup RAISINS

Cream shortening and sugar together. Add egg and beat well. Put baking soda in tomato soup and add water. Sift dry ingredients and add alternately with soup to shortening mixture. Fold in raisins. Pour into a greased 13 x 9 cake pan. Bake at 350° for 45 minutes. Frost with ***Butter-n-Cream Cheese Frosting.***

Butter-n-Cream Cheese Frosting

1/4 lb. BUTTER
8 oz. CREAM CHEESE
1 lb. POWDERED SUGAR
2 tsp. VANILLA

Soften butter and cream cheese. Add powdered sugar and vanilla. Beat until smooth and creamy.

Chocolate Cake

"This cake was a family favorite on my grandmother's farm."

Elaine Hansen—Union Grove

4 squares CHOCOLATE
1 cup WATER
2 cups SUGAR
1/2 cup SHORTENING
4 EGGS
2 tsp. BAKING SODA
1/2 cup SOUR CREAM
2 cups FLOUR

In a double boiler, melt the chocolate and combine with water. Cream together the sugar and shortening, add chocolate mixture, then mix in the eggs one at a time. Combine baking soda and sour cream and blend into sugar mixture, alternating with flour. Pour batter into baking pans and bake at 350° for 40 minutes.

Grandma's Chocolate Christmas Cookies

"I remember visiting grandmother Smith when I was young and it was always a treat when she gave me a plate to go down to the cellar to get these cookies she kept in a stone jar."

Matilda "Stormy" Bobula—Baraboo

8 Tbsp. COCOA
1 cup BOILING WATER
2 cups SHORTENING
2 cups SUGAR
6 EGGS, separated
2 cups MOLASSES
8-9 cups FLOUR
2 tsp. SALT
2 tsp. BAKING POWDER
2 tsp. CLOVES
2 tsp. NUTMEG
2 tsp. CINNAMON

Pour boiling water over cocoa, stir and let cool. Combine cocoa mixture with balance of ingredients (except egg whites) in order listed. Chill dough overnight. Roll out dough and cut out cookies with Christmas cutters. Bake at 375° for 10-15 minutes. Use egg whites in your favorite 7-minute Frosting Recipe and frost cookies when cool.

Mom's Sponge Cake

"This has been our family recipe for shortcake, especially strawberry, for more than 50 years. I was twelve years old the first time my mother let me make it."

Marlene M. Reinders—West Bend

1 cup FLOUR
1 1/4 tsp. BAKING POWDER
3 EGGS, separated
1/2 cup SUGAR
3 Tbsp. COLD WATER

Sift flour, measure, add baking powder and sift again. Beat egg whites until frothy. Gradually beat in sugar, 2 tablespoons at a time, until soft peaks form. Beat egg yolks until thick and lemon colored (about 5 minutes). Add cold water and continue beating until thick. Gently fold in beaten whites. Gradually fold flour into egg yolk mixture, sifting 1/4 cup at a time over the surface. Pour into a 9 x 9 ungreased baking pan and bake at 325° for 40 minutes.

English Christmas Pudding

"At the age of seven, my great, great grandmother, Margaret Capstick Leake, came to America from Yorkshire, England in 1849. This recipe was brought along on that voyage by her mother, also named Margaret."

Linda L. Leake—Palmyra

1 lb. GROUND BEEF SUET
1 lb. WHITE BREAD, crusts removed and cubed
1 lb. BROWN SUGAR
1 lb. WHITE FLOUR
1 lb. DARK RAISINS
1 lb. CURRANTS

4 EGGS
1 pt. SWEET MILK
1 tsp. ground CINNAMON
1 tsp. ground CLOVES
1 tsp. NUTMEG
dash of SALT

Mix all ingredients together in a large bowl. Divide the dough into four (or two) portions, placing each portion in the center of a clean dish towel (not terry cloth) which has been sprinkled with flour. Tie each "bag" with cloth string (do not tie so tightly that there is no room for expansion, or so loosely that the pudding spills out). In a large kettle, steam the pudding bags for 2 1/2 hours (4 hours for two bags) on a rack in 1-2 inches of water. Bring the water to a rolling boil, then reduce heat to maintain a gentle boil. Cover the kettle tightly with lid during the steaming process. Serve with ***Hard Sauce.*** Each bag of a four bag pudding serves 6 to 8. Refrigerate bags and reheat by steaming 30 to 60 minutes depending on size of bags. Pudding may also be frozen. Thaw before reheating.

Hard Sauce

1 cup WATER
1/2 cup SUGAR
2 Tbsp. CORNSTARCH
1/4 cup BUTTER
1/4 cup LEMON JUICE
2 tsp. grated LEMON RIND
dash SALT
2 Tbsp. BRANDY

Place water in a saucepan, add sugar and cornstarch. Stir and bring to a boil. Reduce heat and stir until sauce is clear and thickened (about 5 minutes). Stir in butter, lemon juice, rind and salt. Stir in brandy just before serving. Spoon hot sauce over hot pudding.

Polish Molasses Cookies

"My grandmother's mother told us that this recipe was over 100 years old. She said that it was brought from Poland in the early 1800s."

Mrs. Stella L. Anderson—Portage

Cream together:

1/2 cup MOLASSES (either dark or light)
1 EGG, well-beaten
1/2 cup SUGAR
1/4 cup HOT WATER
1/2 cup SHORTENING

Sift together:

2 1/2 cups FLOUR
1 tsp. BAKING SODA
2 tsp. CINNAMON
1/2 tsp. GINGER
pinch of SALT
1 tsp. NUTMEG
1 tsp. ALLSPICE
1/2 tsp. CLOVES
1 Tbsp. COCOA

Combine creamed and sifted mixtures. Form dough into small balls and place on a cookie sheet about 2 inches apart. Press each with the tines of a fork that has been dipped in sugar. When cool, frost cookies with ***Whipped Cream Frosting.***

Whipped Cream Frosting

1/4 cup FLOUR
1 cup MILK
1/2 cup MARGARINE
1/2 cup SHORTENING
1 cup WHITE SUGAR
2 tsp. VANILLA
pinch of SALT

Combine flour and milk in a saucepan and bring to a simmer. Remove from heat and beat thoroughly. Add the balance of ingredients and mix thoroughly again.

Wisconsin Dells

Tour both the Upper and Lower Dells by boat, or try the Dells Duck Tour which offers land and water tours of the region. Noah's Ark, America's largest waterpark can be found here as well as a Ripley's Believe It or Not! And don't miss the Tommy Bartlett Thrill Show, or the Wax World of the Stars! These and many more exciting opportunities abound.

Rhubarb Bars

"My neighbors who collect maple syrup from their trees every fall, gave me this excellent recipe!"

Mrs. Charlotte Gwinn—Gliddon

2 cups FLOUR
1 cup BUTTER or SHORTENING
2 Tbsp. SUGAR

Cream flour, butter and sugar together. Pat mixture into a 9 x 13 greased baking pan. Bake at 350° for 10 minutes.

3 EGG YOLKS
1 pkg. (8 oz.) CREAM CHEESE, softened
3 cups RHUBARB
1 cup SUGAR
3/4 cup MAPLE SYRUP
3 Tbsp. FLOUR
1/8 tsp. SALT
1/3 cup MILK
1/2 tsp. VANILLA
WHIPPED CREAM

Beat together egg yolks and cream cheese until smooth. Add rhubarb and balance of ingredients (except whipped cream). Pour rhubarb mixture over crust in baking pan and bake at 350° for 40 minutes. Serve with dollops of whipped cream on top.

Popcorn Crunch

"A favorite of children of any age! This recipe was 'Grandma' Diehnelt's delicious answer to storebought confections."

Walter Diehnelt—Honey Acres, Inc., Ashippun

1/2 cup melted BUTTER
1/2 cup HONEY
3 qts. popped POPCORN
1 cup NUTS (your favorites)

Blend butter and honey. Heat until well blended; pour over popcorn-nut mixture. Mix well. Spread onto a cookie sheet in a thin layer. Bake in a preheated 350° oven for 10 to 15 minutes or until crisp.

Recipe Contributors

(Continued next page)

Contributors (continued)

We may live without poetry, music and art;
We may live without conscience, and live without heart;
We may live without friends, we may live without books;
But civilized man cannot live without cooks.

We may live without books, what is knowledge but grieving,
We may live without hope–what is hope but deceiving,
We may live without love, what is passion but pining,
But where is man that can live without dining?

– Owen Meredith

Index

(Continued next page)

Index (continued)

(Continued next page)

Index (continued)

(Continued next page)

Index (continued)

(Continued next page)

Index (continued)

More cookbooks by Golden West Publishers

SALSA LOVERS COOK BOOK

More than 180 taste-tempting recipes for salsas that will make every meal a special event! Salsas for salads, appetizers, main dishes and desserts! Put some salsa in your life! By Susan K. Bollin. More than 250,000 copies in print!

5 1/2 x 8 1/2 — 128 pages . . . $6.95

EASY RECIPES for WILD GAME AND FISH

By hunter-traveler-cook Ferne Holmes. More than 200 "wild" recipes for large and small game, wild fowl, fish, and side dishes. By Ferne Holmes, author of ***Easy RV Recipes.***

5 1/2 x 8 1/2 — 160 pages . . . $6.95

BEST BARBECUE RECIPES

A collection of more than 200 taste-tempting recipes.

• Sauces • Rubs • Marinades • Mops • Ribs • Wild Game • Fish and Seafood • Pit barbecue and more!

5 1/2 x 8 1/2 — 144 pages . . . $6.95

APPLE LOVERS COOK BOOK

Celebrating America's favorite—the apple! 150 recipes for main and side dishes, appetizers, salads, breads, muffins, cakes, pies, desserts, beverages, and preserves: all kitchen-tested!

5 1/2 x 8 1/2 — 120 pages . . . $6.95

THE JOY OF MUFFINS

The International Muffin Cook Book

Recipes for German Streusel, Finnish Cranberry, Italian Amaretto, Greek Baklava, Chinese Almond, Jamaican Banana, Swiss Fondue, microwave section and ten recipes for oat bran muffins . . . 150 recipes in all!

5 1/2 x 8 1/2 — 120 pages . . . $6.95

ORDER BLANK

GOLDEN WEST PUBLISHERS

4113 N. Longview Ave. • Phoenix, AZ 85014
www.goldenwestpublishers.com • **1-800-658-5830** • FAX 602-279-6901

Qty	Title	Price	Amount
	Apple Lovers Cook Book	**6.95**	
	Berry Lovers Cook Book	**6.95**	
	Best Barbecue Recipes	**6.95**	
	Chili-Lovers Cook Book	**6.95**	
	Chip and Dip Lovers Cook Book	**6.95**	
	Easy Recipes for Wild Game & Fish	**6.95**	
	Easy RV Recipes	**6.95**	
	Illinois Cook Book	**6.95**	
	Iowa Cook Book	**6.95**	
	Joy of Muffins	**6.95**	
	Michigan Cook Book	**6.95**	
	Minnesota Cook Book	**6.95**	
	Pumpkin Lovers Cook Book	**6.95**	
	Quick-Bread Cook Book	**6.95**	
	Recipes for a Healthy Life Style	**6.95**	
	Salsa Lovers Cook Book	**6.95**	
	Tequila Cook Book	**7.95**	
	Tortilla Lovers Cook Book	**6.95**	
	Veggie Lovers Cook Book	**6.95**	
	Wisconsin Cook Book	**6.95**	
Shipping & Handling Add:	United States $3.00 Canada & Mexico $5.00—All others $12.00		

☐ My Check or Money Order Enclosed

☐ MasterCard ☐ VISA ($20 credit card minimum)

Total $ __________
(Payable in U.S. funds)

Acct. No. ______________________ Exp. Date __________

Signature ______________________

Name ______________________ Phone __________

Address ______________________

City/State/Zip ______________________

Call for a FREE catalog of all of our titles

This order blank may be photo copied.

2/02

Wis. Ck Bk